THE FURTHER PROPHECIES OF
NOSTRADAMUS:
1985 AND BEYOND

Other books by
Erika Cheetham

THE PROPHECIES OF NOSTRADAMUS

THE PROPHECIES OF NOSTRADAMUS
New Revised and Updated Edition

The Further
PROPHECIES

Translated, Edited and Introduced by

OF NOSTRADAMUS:
1985 and Beyond

ERIKA CHEETHAM

A PERIGEE BOOK

Perigee Books
are published by
The Putnam Publishing Group
200 Madison Avenue
New York, NY 10016

Library of Congress Cataloging in Publication Data

Cheetham, Erika.
  The further prophecies of Nostradamus.

    1. Nostradamus, 1503–1566.   Prophéties.
  2. Prophecies (Occult sciences)   I. Nostradamus,
  1503–1566. Prophéties.   II. Title.
  BF1815.N8C47   1985   133.3   84-26619
  ISBN 0-399-51121-0

Printed in the United States of America

1 2 3 4 5 6 7 8 9 10

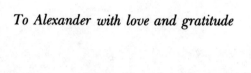

To Alexander with love and gratitude

Contents

PROLOGUE

The manner in which I came across Nostradamus and his famous book of predictions, *Les Prophéties de M. Michel de Nostradamus*, is almost as strange as the many places to which it has since led me over the past twenty years.

I was eighteen, at the beginning of my second year at Oxford, and after Prelims—the examination one took in my day after two terms—I decided to change from reading Modern Languages and opted to study as my main language Langue d'Oc, that is, Ançien Provençal and its dialects. It was a flourishing literary period covering not only the glamour of the troubadour literature, far more of which remains than is generally realized, but also the troubled times of the Cathars and the Albigensians. It wasn't a popular course. It involved a great deal of hard work, a good knowledge of Latin and an interest in etymology, in which I was conspicuous for my lack of ability. For some arbitrary reason known only to God and the Oxford School of Languages, the period extended from the seventh century A.D. to 1492. Ironically, at the time all my contemporaries told me I was mad and that I would never make a career of it!

One sunny autumn afternoon I was sitting in the Taylorian library—the linguist's equivalent to the Bodleian, waiting for a text I had ordered. Eventually a book arrived. It was a tiny volume of about 5 × 3 inches. Opening it I found that it was not the work I had requested but *Les Prophéties de M. Michel de Nostradamus,* printed at Lyons in 1568. I had never heard of Nostradamus, but while waiting for the correct book of Provençal lyrics to arrive I naturally flipped through it. I was making very little sense out of the mingled verses with its polyglot vocabulary when one particular quatrain caught my eye. It was quatrain 24, in the Second of the Ten Centuries (100 verses) into which the book was divided, which incidentally make for difficult concentrated reading. It went as follows:

> *Bestes farouches de faim fleuves tranner,*
> *Plus part du champ encontre Hister sera.*
> *En caige de fer le grand fera traisner,*
> *Quand rien enfant de Germain observera.*

II.24

The name Hister (particularly when printed with

the long, old-fashioned *s* which looks like an *l*)
linked with Germany first caught my interest. I
translated the verse and became quite excited. A
man called Hister linked with Germany and war! It
seemed more than a coincidence when I realized
that it had been written over 400 years earlier.

> *Beasts wild with hunger will cross the rivers, the*
> *greater part of the battle will be against Hitler. He will*
> *cause great men to be dragged in a cage of iron, when the*
> *son of Germany observes no law.*
>
> *II.24*

I continued to read and found several other references to this mysterious Hister—also called the
Captain of the Crooked Cross, the swastika; the
Captain of Greater Germany, the Third Reich.
Then alas, my work arrived and Nostradamus
was relegated to the back of my mind for some
years.

However, I did find time to read James Laver's
excellent if somewhat edited book on Nostradamus
which he wrote at the beginning of the last war, and
later was lucky enough to get to know him well
before his tragic death; but that, like Nostradamus,
was still in the future.

At that time at Oxford I was going through an
acute love affair which ranged from the delirious to
the utterly miserable, which I sincerely believe
helped induce in me a highly perceptive state. I
have since read that ESP researchers have found
that heightened emotions are more likely to pro-

duce this, whereas people receptive to such phenomena as telepathy are preferably in a more
passive frame of mind. Be that as it may. I became
very good at reading hands and the Tarot cards, in
fact so good I began to frighten myself. The cards
or the hands were not important. They were purely
an object on which I could concentrate, just as a
skryer uses a crystal ball, and both the Delphic Oracle and Nostradamus used a bowl of water on a
bronze tripod.

A typical example was one evening at a friend's
room in one of the colleges on the High. I was
asked to tell some fortunes—sing for my supper so
to speak—and one of the guests was a rich Egyp-
tian student. He was about 20 years old. I hardly
knew him except by sight and was amazed when on
taking his hand to be surrounded by a feeling of
deepest gloom and despair, and was momentarily
unable to say anything. I laughed the situation off,
made light of it saying I was feeling tired. Nevertheless the feeling of unease remained. Two days
later I learned that he had flown to Rome for the
weekend, the day after the party, and had been
shot dead at the airport by the irate husband of one
of his mistresses.

I also began to have precognitive dreams which I
mentioned to various close friends, and which
seemed to come true. One was about a friend who
had a serious car crash on the way to London, several days after my dream. The extraordinary thing
was that he didn't own a car and had borrowed one

for the day. Another authenticated dream was just after my marriage. I was living and working with friends down in Kent, as my husband had been drafted with his regiment to the Cameroons. One night I had a vivid dream of his being in a truck which went over a cliff. Communications between us were few and far between as he was often out on jungle patrol for more than a week at a stretch. But I wrote immediately, telling him of the dream and asking him to take care. About ten days later a letter arrived, he hadn't yet received mine, describing how on driving back to camp from dinner with some planter in the jungle, his driver, who had rather too much to drink, nearly took them over a precipice. There were quite a few more dreams of this type and I shall discuss the theory of precognitive dreaming in later chapters. It is an interesting fact that these dreams have all the clarity of a "lucid" dream, but somehow one is well aware that they contain more meaning as one awakes.

One final dream which happened very recently, long after I had become involved with Nostradamus and was becoming more and more involved with the problems of time and space, occurred on June 4th, 1981. I was living in Chelsea at the time and had a vivid dream of a man being shot three times in the head. I recognized the area as being somewhere in Park Lane or Mayfair. I awoke extremely shaken. The experience was so real and terrifying that I telephoned a friend and told him of it. He, being highly practical, without my knowledge wrote down the time of my telephone call. According to his notes I rang at 12:45 A.M., i.e., 11:45 Greenwich Mean Time. Checking next day with Reuters, the attempted assassination of the Israeli Ambassador in Mayfair was first announced at 12:22, then 12:29 and 12:48 G.M.T. The fact that he had been shot in the head was not reported until 3:51 A.M., and only then was it specified that he had been shot three times.

I don't really know what value these dreams and slight precognistic visions have. I am sure that, as Bacon says of predictions, "Men mark them when they hit and not when they miss, as they do again with dreams." My personal experiences have convinced me that somewhere there does lie a positive argument in favor of the possibility of glimpsing the future, whether voluntarily or not. I should like to attempt in this book to air some of the theories and prejudices that now abound, from prophets to cosmologists, and in particular those predictions which relate to the present, 1985, and onward.

An interesting side note. Since writing my original book on Nostradamus as long ago as 1969, based upon a genuine 1568 first edition of his *Prophéties,* which I was lucky enough to obtain after much searching and professional help, I have been approached several times, either by letter or by person, by international figures of some repute, mainly politicians, who have asked me to interpret various of Nostradamus' quatrains with reference to themselves or their countries. This has been an almost impossible task, because they only wished to hear palatable things; the same dilemma as that which faced the astrologer employed by Goebbels, Hans Ernst Krafft, when he was asked to predict Hitler's future fortune and the progress of the war. Others I found impossible to help, simply not understanding, from my knowledge of Nostradamus, and his use of puns and keywords, how they could relate a particular quatrain or quatrains to themselves. It has never ceased to amaze me that this sixteenth century philosopher, doctor, astrologer and astronomer such as Michel de Nostradamus, could cause important men of this century, often with the destiny of millions of people in their hands, to send for me, or come to see me, genuinely believing he could possibly have foretold their futures. Perhaps a fitting summary of this book can be found in a letter written by Wittgenstein when he had completed his *Tractatus Logico-philosophicus*.

"My work consists of two parts: the one presented here plus all that I have not written. And it is precisely the second part that is the important one."

1 IS PREDICTION POSSIBLE?

I suppose that in trying to decide whether valid prediction is possible, one has to attempt to define one's terms. Is a prediction valid if a sufficiently large number of people believe that it is? Does one need some more objective, less involved test of accuracy? If so, in what manner and by whom shall the tests of accuracy be carried out? These questions are easy to ask and hard to answer.

I feel that if a sufficient number of people believe in a prophet, then the accuracy of his predictions can become of secondary importance. Many followers will decide, when the predictions are no longer rationally tenable, that they have misunderstood them and look for different interpretations. This can be seen clearly enough in the early years of some spiritual religions. Faith is made stronger especially when the predictions are written in obscure language, because the author was inspired or in some form of trance, possibly from a desire to avoid trouble with religious authorities (as was true for Nostradamus). It was very rarely done in my experience from a wish to confuse or mislead. If prophets were confused they were self-deluded.

Anyone can verify political events and natural disasters. On a more trivial scale people predict the winners of races and movements in stock prices. Predictions that concern personal events, including diagnosis and cure, seem to be of insufficient interest in a book of this nature for them to be included, though several prophets (including Nostradamus) have been well known as healers. Therefore I have largely excluded both of these. For the same reasons and also for the sake of clarity I have excluded astrology, horoscopes and similar subjects, which should not be taken as necessarily indicating either belief or disbelief on my part.

I thought for a long time before deciding to put the word "prediction" rather than the word "prophecy" at the head of this chapter. The word "prophecy" has for me strong religious connotations—memories of the Old Testament prophets speaking of the wrath to come. Prediction is more secular, but does not exclude religion, which is partly why I chose it. But can one say that predictions are made by predictors? It may be strictly logical, but it sounds wrong. To me a predictor is some kind of computer that predicts the course of a ballistic missile or hopefully tomorrow's weather. Illogically, therefore, predictions must be made by prophets, which is why I use that word throughout the book.

Prophets are not necessarily the inspired men of popular vision. They can be cool, rational, calculating, even lacking in religious belief. H. G. Wells's *The Shape of Things to Come* is just as much a work of prophecy as the many predictions made by Jeane Dixon, a devout Catholic. *1984*, written by the socialist George Orwell, is as prophetic as the Centuries of Nostradamus, written in a trance-like state of inspiration by a very different kind of man.

Writers such as Nietzsche, Burckhardt, Spengler, Toynbee and Sorokin don't contain sufficient relatively precise predictions for this type of book. Nor do most Christian and socialist apologists, who I feel have insufficient respect for things as they really are.

I obviously accept that some valid predictions are possible, or I should not be writing this book. I hope in the course of it to convince the skeptical reader that prediction can be possible and is surprisingly frequent and successful for all its expected uncertainties. Why a higher standard of proof should be expected from it by the reader than he might get from a work of science or history, such as the Old Testament, seems unreasonable. I believe that prediction is valid and should be taken and used much more seriously than it is.

Prediction exists in the first place because there is a demand for it; "demand creates its own supply," which every modern consumer knows, and indeed, can scarcely avoid. The simplest form of prediction can hardly be distinguished from advice, requiring a yes or no, an answer to a simple question, such as "Should I marry such and such a man?" or "Should I make a journey to such a place in such a month?," and often enough, "Will this business venture be successful?." Many of the questions put to oracles in ancient Greece were of this type, but the positive and negative answers were provided in several different ways. The petitioner basically believed in the benevolence of the oracle, and that better results would flow from following the advice given than from not following it. In one sense, if the oracle's statement was definitely followed, benefits might follow—they were never guaranteed. But by negatively ignoring the oracle the questioner was placing himself in a position of considerable danger. Oracles were often double-tongued; misinterpretation could be fatal. A good example is the experience of Philip of Macedon, father of Alexander the Great, when consulting the Delphic Oracle. The Oracle uttered the cryptic words: "Wreathed is the bull for the war and the end fulfilled. And the slayer too is ready." The king misread the statement as meaning he would be victorious but the ensuing battle led to his death.

Interestingly enough, inspired prediction does not necessarily imply precognition by a human mind of a specific event. A prophet may feel no more than . . . let us call them good or bad vibrations, favorable or unfavorable feelings about a particular person or specific situation about which he cannot be more elaborate. Prediction may be based on elaborate procedures that have been established for hundreds of years, like the Chinese method of divination, the I Ching, or African methods of throwing bones, or horoscopes based on astrological calculations related to the time and place of birth of an individual or an organization.

Horoscopes can be relevant in the oddest of circumstances. I have a friend whose wedding took place on June 24th, 1950. As the wedding party was going on, North Korean troops invaded South Korea. With a secular horoscope like that, the marriage had no chance of success. My friend was not surprised, indeed rather expected it to last less than two years. And he was right. What a wedding gift!

Some inspired prophets differentiate between predictions that are inevitable and others that are avoidable. It seems quite a common phenomenon. What is rarer are those predictors who can continuously and confidently perceive this distinction. A well-known example is Jeane Dixon, whom I shall discuss further on in this book. For her, the assassination of President Kennedy was inevitable, whereas that of his brother, Senator Robert Kennedy, was definitely avoidable. I shall write later about a prophecy by Nostradamus, which I interpret to predict the violent deaths of three brothers of the Kennedy family, the third to come being that of Senator Edward Kennedy. Probably one needs to be closer in time to the events predicted than was Nostradamus to make that distinction between inevitable and avoidable. If he had predicted only avoidable events his reputation would have perished long ago, at the hands of those who had survived dangers. I wonder what would have happened to Jeane Dixon's reputation if she had been able to get her warnings through to Robert Kennedy and if he had taken notice of them? I believe she also tried to warn Martin Luther King, Jr., but he was a man, in my opinion, who had taken his own path long before and who would not be deflected from a self-imposed fate.

There are times when prophets should act like their predecessors in the Old Testament, by giving warnings of disasters to come, hoping that appropriate actions might be taken. Sadly, most are too scared of public ridicule. I would like to think, or perhaps I should say believe, that George Orwell's *1984* is more of a dreadful warning of what *could* happen than an accurate prophecy of what *will* happen in England. Sir John Hackett's *The Third World War* should also be looked upon as a prediction that one would like to see proven wrong. I have the same view about the prophecies of millennial destruction by Nostradamus and Jeane Dixon—let us hope that they are wrong. I feel that this century has great disasters on the horizon but they have nothing to do with A.D. 2000. This brings us to the paradoxical point of view that a prediction is "successful" if the undesirable events in it do *not* come to pass but equally, then, the prophet is not vindicated. Possibly the most committed ones have a vested interest in disaster?

In the case of predictions about disasters, natural or man-made, it is useful to distinguish between an event and its consequences, which can be mitigated by precautionary measures. There are obvious practical difficulties, in that those who have dreams or visions or other precognitions of such events can be specific about time and place only in a few instances. It may be possible to develop methods of precognition and more effective networks for bringing disaster predictions to the attention of the authorities concerned.

Some theorists, among them J. W. Dunne, believed that a faculty of precognition was not at all unusual and might even be normal. Whatever truth that has for small-scale personal events, I do not believe it to be true for the larger-scale public domain of events. The ability to make inspired predictions on the grand scale for centuries ahead is very rare indeed. Nostradamus is almost unique in the scope of his foresight. Hence his title "The King Among Prophets."

Precognitive gifts in an individual may last for many years or quickly fade away. It does not always follow that a prophet with a good record of predictions, inspired or rational, will be able to continue being successful. As I have shown in this chapter, there are difficulties in defining success or validity.

My aim in this book is to be illustrative rather than exhaustive, to show that there have been and are successful prophets and to demonstrate that valid prediction is possible, rather than to write a history of prophecy. That admitted, we should examine theories of time that are consistent with it, and various ways in which predictions manifest themselves to those who experience them, before going on to Nostradamus and other prophets of our recent past and near future.

2   THEORIES OF TIME

I hope to have shown in this book and in my previous book on the predictions of Nostradamus that his record as a prophet is sufficiently good for him to be taken seriously, even by those who profess to be skeptical about such matters. It is true that his record is far from perfect, that those who sought to interpret him in the past did not all come to the same conclusions as mine on certain quatrains. No doubt there will be further changes in interpretations in the future, partly when hitherto obscure quatrains become clearer as events unfold in the real world. Prophecy and magic are still felt by many people to be not wholly respectable. Why therefore do they unconsciously demand a higher standard of proof for the validity of prophecies made more than 400 years ago than they would demand for the truth of a revealed religion—if they believe in one—or of a secular explanation of events, such as Marxism. I rather feel that prophets suffer from our double standards!

Given acceptance of the adequacy of a prophet's record, and the natural desire of every man, woman and child to have an explanation, whether in terms of why or how, some investigation of theories of time must find a place in this book. An exhaustive history of the many theories of time, religious and philosophical, scientific and literary, could easily run into hundreds of pages and leave one none the wiser for reading them. Here my aim is much more limited. I shall attempt to present and discuss some of these theories of time which may provide us with partial explanations for the existence of successful prophecies and prophets, and for Nostradamus in particular.

I propose to limit this examination to the Western world, from its Greco-Roman and Christian origins onward; therefore, I will exclude Eastern religions such as Islam, Buddhism, other religions of India, Japan and China and precolonial religions of Africa and America. For many of these parts of the world the cyclical or reversible nature of time is self-evident. They do not need any special theories to explain prediction. It is part of their lives, and Nostradamus' sixteenth-century neo-Catholicism would be nothing but an intrusion.

We have become so accustomed, in English and many other European languages, to using such expressions as "a long time" and "a short time" that it no longer strikes us as odd that we should be using adjectives relating to distance and apply them to time. Is it possible that in our unconscious, our subconscious minds we have for centuries accepted the idea of a four-dimensional time continuum? That would certainly be one explanation for the muddling up of our adjectives. Did Einstein simply dredge up from the collective unconscious and put into mathematical terms something that has been accepted without being fully known or understood for centuries, if not for millennia? I think one could say with P. G. Wodehouse, "the mind boggles."

Most people still use watches that show the time with hands that mark it by their position against numbers and dials. The same is true of clocks. The younger generation, on the whole, prefer digital watches or clocks, many driven by very small electric batteries, in which the passage of time is marked by sudden changes in visible figures, without continuous movement. I believe that people who use watches and clocks with revolving indicators unconsciously assume that time is primarily cyclical, at least for seconds, minutes and hours, whereas those who become accustomed to digital time indicators gradually develop an unconscious perception of time as primarily linear. The gap between generations is strongly indicated here and could be one which may never be reversed.

In turn this presumably predisposes people to regard larger units of time as either cyclical or linear, not necessarily based on cause and effect; it often happens that people with cyclical perceptions of time prefer cyclical indicators of time. Whatever the relations between perceptions and indicators, there are and have been for at least the last two and a half thousand years continuous differences of opinion, and arguments between believers in cyclical time and believers in linear time. Even now, some cosmologists believe that the universe began with a big bang some 10,000 to 15,000 million years ago while others maintain that the universe has always existed and that creation is continuous.

A few years ago I read in the *Times Literary Supplement* a review of *The First Three Minutes*, which purported to describe a "big bang" beginning of the universe. It was apparently a serious scientific work. The reviewer mentioned some simple mathematical proofs included by the author. It seemed to me a breathtaking exercise in credulity, more farfetched than the most extreme assertions or revelations about time to be found in Eastern religions. But it was readily accepted by scientists because of its being presented in explanatory terms currently fashionable and therefore credible. We used to leave cosmology, which deals with the structure and history of the universe as a whole, to theologians and philosophers. Currently we leave it to astronomers and mathematicians.

In a book on cosmology published about ten years ago Sir Bernard Lovell expressed the view that recent discoveries had uncovered more problems than solutions about the universe. This makes a layman like myself feel that the *effect* of research, scientific, historical, literary or anything else, just adds to the sum of human ignorance. It doesn't, despite any intention to the contrary, add to what we know. Do researchers write for themselves and their brotherhood? It seems like it a great deal of the time.

Christians, however, perhaps through the Hebrew foundations of their religion, find the concept of endless repetitive cycles repugnant and unacceptable. These concepts are also found in Eastern philosophies and later in the independently developed religions of the Mayas and the Aztecs of southern America.

In contrast to the Greeks, more particularly to Aristotle, St. Augustine took a more subjective view of time, seeing it as experienced in the mind of man, though not denying time some external reality as well. He states in his *Confessions:*

> *Perhaps it might be said rightly that there are three times: a time present of things past, a time present of things present and a time present of things future. For these three do coexist somehow in the soul, for otherwise I could not see them.*

> *The time present of things past is memory; the time present of things present is direct experience; the time present of things future is expectation.*

> *Confessions XI.20*

The three times present do not, unfortunately, allow for the possibility of valid prophecy based on some kind of foreknowledge of the future, for the time present of things future is only expectation. According to St. Augustine, there is no way for the mind of man to have direct knowledge of eternity. He also argues explicitly that time is linear in nature and that the whole history of the universe is single, irreversible, unrepeatable, from its creation by God through the life of Jesus Christ as its central event to the end of the world. He understands Earth as the only planet in the universe on which "thinking" man exists. Until Kant, St. Augustine's exposition of the subjective theory of time was unequaled.

But by the early sixteenth century general comprehension of time had veered away from that of St. Augustine toward a more astronomical approach. The best and most interesting examples, loosely contemporaneous with Nostradamus, were Luther and Calvin. Both were even more hostile than the Catholic Church to Copernicus' theory (for which he was severely persecuted) that the earth revolved daily around its own axis, and annually around the sun. This hostility between astronomy and the Christian religion had greatly lessened by the time Newton propounded his belief in absolute space and time. I should like to introduce here one of my favorite authors, Sir Thomas Browne, an act of self-indulgence, I admit, probably as a garnish to the cake. In his *Religio Medici*

(I/59) he says, "the world was before the creation and at an end before it had a beginning, and thus I was dead before I was alive . . ." Perhaps this is ironic, certainly a paradox, but from the viewpoint of timeless eternity in which all things past and present exist, it is a very useful theory to help one understand valid prophecy, with the one proviso that one accepts that these imponderables are, or can be, known.

Progressing, if that is the right word, to modern times, one is faced with two great personalities, Bergson and Einstein. The former connects time with intuition and space with intellect, rather like C. G. Jung. Einstein's famous theory of relativity substitutes space-time for space and time and events for particles of matter. Two events could be contemporaneous—all depending upon the observer. In fact, his notion of a fourth dimension dates back at least 100 years earlier, but only since about 1920 have writers, such as Orwell in his novel, *1984*, made much use of the space-time continuum theory for literature. Bergson is really more mythological than philosophical. The most important statement of his philosophy is that future events do not exist at all. This was necessary for his vindication of freedom and free will. Unscientific he may have been, but unscientific theories are *not* necessarily invalid. As they say, "You pays your money and you takes your choice." With two such diverse philosophies one has but little option.

J. W. Dunne is altogether a different problem. It

is hard to know whether one should treat his theories as scientific or analogic, although Dunne himself definitely saw them as scientific and proven. I first came into contact with J. W. Dunne's *An Experiment With Time* when up at Oxford. The copy I bought then is still in my possession, much worn, lacking covers, heavily annotated in red and blue ink. I used to think that his theories of time, apparently with a scientific basis, were helpful in explaining the possibility and nature of valid prophecy. Now I am a good deal less sure about him, probably as a result of studying other theories of time, many of which stand up better to critical examination than those of Dunne. His ideas now seem to me to be more like analogies and to fall somehow between the two stools labeled "literary and political views of time" and "scientific and philosophical theories of time." But Dunne's views are still the subject of a good deal of popular attention and some reference to his theories is really almost a moral obligation.

I do not find that any of Dunne's assertions are proven. They concern precognition in a limited way, and also dreams, which he claims to have roughly equal resemblances to the past and to the future. In my judgment, neither his results nor his theories are of much value in attempting to explain prophecy and prediction.

Dunne's views are still popular and believed by many to be valid and important. Modern cosmology seems to me to provide more useful and interesting guidance. Scientific understanding is said to advance only by proposing theories which can be submitted to empirical tests. If a theory passes early tests, then its proponents must make more and more forecasts that can be tested. Sooner or later, of course, every theory must fail a test or be unable to account for some data or events. It is then, scientifically, held to be disproved, invalid. I cannot help thinking that this approach is far too destructive, too rigorous, even in the relatively narrow domains of human experience where scientists feel sufficiently confident to formulate theories and make predictions. Almost all reviews of books on philosophy seem to be written with demolition in mind, yet books on revealed and secular religions such as Christianity and Marxism are as a rule reviewed much more sympathetically.

In the face of the enormous uncertainties of cosmology and philosophy, some scientists seem to have abandoned the closed rigidities of the scientific approach for something a good deal more open-minded; indeed, the professorial title of one of the greater ones, Professor Rees, includes that of Experimental Philosophy. His suggestion that we should not take "an over-restrictive view of what constitutes an observer" leads me to propose that we should also be more broad-minded in what we think it appropriate to observe, and in the kinds of explanations or observations that we are prepared to accept. This is certainly essential with prophecy.

If time can be accepted as a variable for the convenience of cosmologists and mathematicians, it seems to me that people such as myself can also legitimately make more relaxed assumptions. Why can't time accelerate? Implicitly, time is invariant, a second is a second is a second. But there is plenty of evidence that that is not true for subjective time, time in the mind, a factor of vital importance when considering the aims of this book, time as understood by a prophet.

Many of us have experienced a sudden deceleration of time, a change in its apparent velocity. I have experienced this sometimes when on a long drive: the speed of my car, as shown by the speedometer, has not changed, yet there is a sudden slowing down of time, everything passes at half speed. Working late at night after a long day sometimes produces deceleration in my sense of time, when my rate of work goes up sharply and the number of errors goes down. But any acceleration back to the normal velocity of time is more gradual.

We should recall also one of the postulates of relativity theory, however difficult it may be to accept. If one of a pair of twins goes off at high velocity away from the earth, returning a few years later, then his age when he gets back to the earth will not be the same as that of the twin who has stayed there. Here we have something more than mere change in the velocity of time. We have overlapping times. There will be a certain biological interval that lies in the future for one twin, which the other twin has already experienced. It is rather like the "loop of time" referred to by a character in one of T. S. Eliot's plays, *The Family Reunion*. One could say, by analogy, that one of the twins mentioned above has experienced such a loop in time, denied to the other twin. Probably the existence of such loops is one of the preconditions for valid prophecy, which does not rule out the possibility of other explanations.

Perhaps another precondition, additional rather than alternative, is some form of telepathic communication, without specifying at this stage what the transmitter and receiver might be. Telepathic communication between a minority of human beings has, I believe, been sufficiently proven for me to take it for granted. The combination of a relativistic loop in time with a human receiver and whatever one wishes to specify as transmitter of telepathic messages, can provide at least a possible explanatory mechanism for precognition and prophecy, more valid than Dunne and no more fantastic than modern cosmology.

Some years ago I saw a television play: *The Stone Tapes*, in which some scientists attempt to account for the appearance of a ghost, reenacting the death of a housemaid, with a theory that the original event was in some way recorded in the stones of the building, and that under appropriate conditions the original recording would be replayed, aurally and visually. Possibly a mechanism of this sort and a loop in time would provide an explanation for valid prophecy, assuming a telepathic communication from source to receiver. Whether the source is to be physical or some kind of divine presence or lesser spirit is very much a matter of opinion.

It seems to me that some kind of cyclical theory of time, providing for recurrence and anticipation, is necessary to explain the possibility of valid predictions or prophecies, such as those by Nostradamus. Whether the existence of successful prophecies, which I regard as proven, is sufficient evidence in itself for a cyclical theory of time, is something outside the scope of this book and certainly beyond my competence to argue. But to assert that there can be no valid theory of time which does not account for the existence of verified prophecy appears to me no less scientific than many assertions of modern cosmology.

Benson Herbert, a British scientist attempting to find explanations for precognition and prophecy, has evolved the idea that the "present" in subjective time has a short duration when one is fully alert, and a much longer duration when one is asleep. In a state of trance, absence from the physical world, the "present" may stretch over years. Precognition is a function of lack of attention to the physical world. Following Dunne, one might expect the "present" to extend equally into the future and into the past, continuing his theory that the content of dreams contains links to past and future in roughly equal proportions.

There neither are nor will be final answers or perfect theories of time that can adequately explain precognition and prophecy. Some theories seem more applicable than others. None really deny their existence.

Let us leave to St. Augustine the last word on time: "What, then, is time? If no one asks me, I know what it is. If I wish to explain it to him who asks me, I do not know."

3 VISION, REVELATION, TRANCE AND DREAMS

All these concepts—vision, revelation, trance and dreams—*can* yield predictions that are more or less inspired, as distinct from those that obviously derive their source from reason and calculation. They do not *necessarily* yield predictions, which can in any case arise in other ways. Should one take these four concepts and think of them as sources, methods, channels, media for predictions? No single description is wholly appropriate, nor wholly inappropriate. The concepts themselves are by no means distinct, though in general they are mutually exclusive.

I understand a "vision" in this context to mean something seen in a waking state in or outside the mind, whether real in some sense or an hallucination, which may last a moment or be continued intermittently over hours, days, weeks or longer. It is not solely or necessarily visible, for the appearance in the mind or externally very often includes one or more voices or other sounds. Thus a "vision" is typically both visual and aural, but can be one or the other. I cannot find a more suitable word than vision, which unfortunately implies that seeing is the primary sense engaged. The senses of touch, taste, and smell sometimes play subsidiary roles in visions. Certainly Nostradamus "heard" voices and possibly "read" words in his visions created in the bowl of water on the bronze tripod.

"Revelation" is limited to messages that are accepted by their recipient as coming directly or indirectly from some divine source, God or a god or goddess, perhaps from a saint, or from a prophet no longer alive. It does not necessarily follow that other people will accept the divine origin of a given revelation. Even the Catholic Church treats them with a certain care.

"Trance" is a state similiar to sleep but with some obvious differences excluding such states as unconsciousness, concussion, seizures, but including deep hypnosis. In prediction or prophecy trance is usually self-induced, though someone in trance may need the help of another to return to a normal waking state. What happened in trance may or may not be remembered afterward, the former sometimes being called an ecstatic trance and the latter a mediumistic trance. A person in trance will usually speak or communicate in other ways. Sensitivity to pain will be reduced or suspended. Edgar Cayce is the supreme modern example of this.

"Dreams" as such need no definition, only a limitation for the purposes of this book to occurrences in a sleeping state, similar occurrences in a waking state being described as visions.

Some examples of well attested visionaries include Joan of Arc (1411–1431). She may have known of a prophecy that France would be restored by an armed virgin from Lorraine, which she was. In 1422 the infant Henry VI of England, son of Henry V of England and the French princess Catherine, was proclaimed King of France at St. Denis. Charles the Dauphin was recognized as king in some parts of France. From 1424 onward Joan felt a sense of mission to free France from the English, urged on by the visionary voices of St. Michael, St. Catherine and St. Margaret. In 1429 she set forth to the court of the Dauphin and, after her authenticity and chastity had been accepted, she led an army to relieve Orléans from the English. She was successful. Other victories followed. In July 1429 she stood beside the Dauphin as he was crowned Charles VII of France. In May 1430 she was captured by the Burgundians. Having incurred by her visions the hostility of the Inquisition and the University of Paris, she was burned at the stake in May 1431. The sentence passed on her was revoked by the Pope in 1456, and in the twentieth century she was accepted as a saint. Memory of her fate no doubt cautioned Nostradamus.

St. Teresa of Avila (1515–1582) was more fortunate in her visions. They began in 1554, after twenty years as a Carmelite nun. Some visions were of Christ, others of hell in all its horrors. She founded some thirty convents and monasteries in her lifetime. Perhaps it was fortunate for her that her visions did not relate to secular affairs. She was held in great honor by King Philip II of Spain and became a saint within fifty years of her death.

The American prophetess Jeane Dixon clearly distinguishes between visions and revelations, the latter being inevitable whereas the former are not. As she writes in her book *My Life and Prophecies,* on page 122:

"*. . . it was not because he had to die . . . all of the visions I received about the pending death of Senator Robert F. Kennedy were reflections of thoughts of men. Men planned his death, not God . . . he chose to die.*"

On the same page Mrs. Dixon reports a dream of Joseph Kennedy, father of the Senator, of the late President and of Senator Edward Kennedy, being embraced by the patriarch Job, whose misfortunes and unshakeable belief in God are well known to all readers of the Bible. Mrs. Dixon also describes in her book the precognition she received, not by revelation, that Martin Luther King, Jr. would be assassinated as the result of a Communist conspiracy. In many places in her book Mrs. Dixon speaks of visions; in connection with the Apollo space program, in anticipation of race riots, about the Kennedy family and the Soviet Union.

The American prophet Edgar Cayce also sometimes had visions, such as one of the chariot of the Lord and his horseman, a childhood vision of an angel from whom he asked the gift of healing, but it was not his normal way of getting psychic readings.

The friend whose dream of July 1966 I refer to later in this chapter had a vision in 1978, when staying overnight in a European capital. A pleasant female voice in his mind told him the title of a play, in which there were six characters (the parallel with Pirandello's play occurred to my friend), and informed him that he was going to write it. His plea of incompetence was swept aside with the assurance that all he had to do was write down what the characters told him. Eight characters, not six, invaded his mind the following evening, saying that they had decided on two plays rather than one. Five weeks later, the plays were completed, to his relief and the satisfaction of the characters; there had been anxious moments when the characters invaded his mind in the middle of business meetings, causing him to temporarily lose track of what he was saying, but the characters were sufficiently well-mannered to withdraw. After five years and about three-quarters of a million words in plays, novels and short stories, my friend accepts that he must write for part of each year, whether or not any of it is suitable for publication, so that he may pursue other activities in peace and sanity.

His vision was visual and aural, totally within his mind. There has been no recurrence of the same intensity after the first five weeks. It may or not be a precognitive vision of a career as a writer, something that had not previously had a place in his plans or ambitions for the future.

I have only once experienced what might be termed a vision or hallucination. I was eight years old but still remember it with extreme clarity to this day. It occurred during the early spring of 1947, in Wales, when the great snows of that year were still up to the bedroom walls at one side of our house. I was in bed during daylight—I must have been ill—the curtains were open and the bed faced toward the window. The room had a central light hanging from the ceiling. For no apparent reason suddenly a single small wing—like that of a cherub or seraph—flew gently three times around the light from left to right and then vanished. I felt no particular emotion, certainly no fear, and didn't mention it to anyone for many years. It held no meaning for me then and I have never found any significance in it since. The only things of interest are the clarity of the actual event and the way it has remained in my memory. No doubt it has helped me to accept the reality of other people's visions. My mother has since assured me I had a very mild infection and that there was no possibility of my being delirious.

In Old Testament times prophecy was taken for granted, and for a time in the early Christian Church it was accepted that God continually conferred His gift upon prophets and teachers. Each local church had its prophet, who was directly inspired by the Holy Spirit and therefore not under the control of its congregation. Inspiration sometimes took the form of ecstasy or it might be restrained by reason. As time passed the permanent officials of the Church came to dislike prophets; the genuine prophets came to dislike the dishonest rogues who had set up as prophets; some congregations resented the harsh conditions imposed on them by the sterner prophets. Order had to be brought out of chaos. It was decreed that no prophet might speak in ecstasy, which came from the devil, and that true prophets could not accept gifts. A new theory was evolved, that all divine revelations were summed up in the Apostles and in their writings, that is, in the New Testament. No further revelations, visions or other forms of guidance were required or would be admitted by the Church, which in this way got its own prophets under control and differentiated itself more clearly from other religions by about 200 A.D. Occasional prophetic utterances were not ruled out, but they could never be on the same level as the Old and New Testaments. Deviations could be heretical or the work of the devil. It was on this theory that the Inquisition based many of its tenets. From time to time thereafter revelations got out of control and new sects were formed.

Because revelation and magic were frowned upon by the hierarchy of the Church for many centuries, prophets such as Nostradamus had to express themselves in obscure languages. One wonders how many prophets before and since have suppressed their prophecies or predictions, to avoid persecution and possible death at the hands of the Inquisition or some similar institution, whose operations were of course not limited to Spain.

The American prophetess Jeane Dixon is a devout Roman Catholic. It is significant of the greater tolerance of the Church nowadays that she can claim to receive revelations. Quoting from her book *My Life and Prophecies,* we find on pages 60 and 61:

> *To me a revelation is God's hand resting on me, revealing what is to take place, and it is an experience that is completely different. . . . All of my revelations deal with international situations. They are never intended for one person as an individual . . . Whatever God reveals in those revelations must come to pass. These are not man-made plans; they are either the will of God or God allows them to happen. In the case of the assassination of President John Kennedy, the knowledge of his death came to me in a revelation, and there was nothing I could do to stop the murder.*

If I have understood Jeane Dixon's book correctly, her prediction of a split in the Catholic Church has come to her as a vision or telepathic message. It does not represent the will of God and will not necessarily happen. Perhaps that is also true of her prediction (page 157) of a Pope who "will be the last one ever to reign as singular head of the Church." Certainly the Vatican appears highly sensitive to popular opinion these days. Mrs. Dixon's visions (I believe that to be the right word, after reading her book) of the coming of the anti-christ have some parallel to the predictions of Nostradamus, and are therefore discussed later in this book. Similarly her revelation of "The Child from the East" (her choice of words, page 177), whom she sees as the "actual person of the Anti-Christ," the one who will deceive the world in Satan's name (page 187) is discussed later. According to Mrs. Dixon, this child was born about 1962, but we should not expect much awareness of his presence until he is twenty-nine or thirty years old. But in the end, God and the righteous win.

The American prophet Edgar Cayce went into a trance state for all his prophetic readings, even to interpret his own dreams and those of other people, often showing as in other readings an astonishing familiarity with the circumstances of the dreamer. People came to him as a rule for advice about future action, so that naturally the emphasis in his interpretations of dreams was on their precognitive or prophetic contents. A considerable body of interpretation had accumulated by the time of Cayce's death. Fortunately the material was preserved and is still being studied and analyzed. He believed that he had some kind of direct access to a universal mind, perhaps similar to Jung's Collective Unconscious, and read daily from the Bible. He had occasional visions too, but for Cayce going into a trance was clearly his chosen method of making predictions. Within the trance, hypnosis played a part in getting his psychic readings, because it was normally someone else who suggested what he should do and look for and later woke him up from his trance.

Trance induction was in classical times a respected method of obtaining valid prophecies, and rather similar methods have been used more recently by Aleister Crowley and by initiates of modern witch cults, for rather different purposes. Aldous Huxley has written of the value of tom-tom music and hallucinogenic drugs such as mescaline for inducing trances.

Investigations of mediumistic trances by respectable organizations such as the Society for Psychical Research appear to lend some support for the ancient theories of possession, by good spirits or the devil or whatever the observers choose to believe in. Naturally this does not meet with the total approval of established churches.

Nostradamus' method of divination, which will be discussed in detail later in the book, might be described as a self-induced state of trance in which he experiences visions.

In Freud's view, all dreams should be seen as wish-fulfillment, more specifically as the fulfillment of sexual wishes. For Adler, all dreams are concerned with the urge to power, with questions of inferiority and superiority between human beings. Jung sees dreams as manifestations from the personal and collective unconscious that are complementary to conscious life, more concerned with the immediate and remote past than with the future. None of these theories is of much value in discussing the rôle of dreams in prediction and precognition.

The well-known dream of Joseph in Egypt is one piece of evidence that such a rôle was taken for granted in antiquity. Plato believed that dreams could be prophetic visions, and the Stoic philosophers thought that they could be a channel for divine revelation. In Greece, dreams that came to enquirers when they slept in the precincts of a temple were thought to be particularly valuable. Thirty miles from Athens there are still to be seen the remains of an oracular shrine the Amphiareion, including a room 360 feet long in which people paid to spend the night that they might receive inspired dreams. At other sanctuaries dreams were thought to be valuable in the diagnosis and cure of illness.

Predictions of natural disasters, often from dreams, have been and are frequent. It is not clear to what extent these are deductions from intelligent observation, and how much they are from more or less inspired sources. J. W. Dunne was by no means the only man to dream about the explosion of Mount Pelée in the West Indies. Many people reported dreams of the Tay Bridge disaster in Scotland in the nineteenth century. More recently, many had premonitions of the Aberfan disaster in South Wales, when a colliery tip suddenly collapsed and buried part of a mining town, including one of the child victims, who related it to her uncomprehending parents the day before she died.

Although the theory of time expounded by J. W. Dunne in his *An Experiment in Time* appears to me to be of doubtful validity, some of the things that he has written on dreams in that book are worth recalling. In the appendix to the third edition he collected the records of eighty-eight dreams by seven "subjects," as he called them, one of them being himself. Each subject searched a period of two and a half months, both before and after each dream, for incidents in his waking life that bore some resemblance to the dream. In total Dunne recorded, within the specified time limits, fourteen resemblances to the past, and twenty resemblances to the future. He regarded these results as conclusive evidence for the existence of precognition, although he adds, "There is no evidence that I possess a special faculty for precognition." He states his belief that "dreams were composed of images of past experience and images of future experience blended together in approximately equal proportions." Elsewhere in the book he reaches the conclusion that similar effects are observable in waking life, and that such effects (waking and sleeping) are quite normal and experienced by many people.

Dreams recorded elsewhere in his book suggest that Dunne was being unduly modest about his own faculty for precognition. Even if one restricts one's attention to events that may be described as public, appearing in newspapers after his dreams, Dunne records precognitive dreams of five major incidents.

> —*the Fashoda incident in the Sudan, 1898*
> —*the volcanic eruption in Martinique, 1902*
> —*a factory fire near Paris, 1904*
> —*an accident to the "Flying Scotsman" train, 1914*
> —*the bombardment of Lowestoft by the German fleet, 1915*

Colin Wilson quotes from Tom Lethbridge's book, *The Pendulum of Dreams*, where he tried to imitate J. W. Dunne in his *An Experiment with Time*, to see if he could produce paranormal information. Using Dunne's technique and keeping a notebook by his bed, he found that many of his dreams distinctly provided knowledge of future events, albeit not as sensational as Dunne's dreams of earthquakes and volcanoes. (In fact a phenomenon that has happened to me many times in my life is that I have woken suddenly in the night and known exactly what time it was before putting on the light and checking, exactly as Dunne did in the "watch" incident. And I was right. I did not have a clock with luminous hands, nor do I normally wear my watch in bed. However, over the past year or so this faculty seems to have almost left me.) Like many of Lethbridge's precognitive dreams it seemed to be an almost useless gift. I cannot wake myself to order as many people claim. These precognitive dreams and flashes of "insight" into the future or the past seldom contain any personal significant meaning. But that does not mean we can dismiss them altogether. They certainly happen, but we do not seem to have the "key" for controlling this state of higher "perception," although some of the Eastern religions seem to comprehend it better than we do in the West.

Another interesting factor about dream prediction is that it very seldom, if ever, benefits the dreamer. If it is a recognizable dream, as was mine of the attempted assassination of the Israeli ambassador, it was impossible for me to warn anyone of *whom* it was that was killed. The event was played out like a TV newsreel without a sound track for explanation, except for the noises of the three shots.

But there is the famous exception of Lord Kilbracken, who as a result of his dreams did make a financial profit, and ended up as racing columnist on the *Daily Mirror*. In 1946—John Godley, as he was then known—dreamed that he was reading a newspaper and read the names of two horses: Bindler and Juladdin. When he and his friends checked the papers next morning he found two horses of those names were running that day and they decided to risk a bet. Both horses won. This happened again some weeks later in Ireland, and again in July 1946. He dreamed several more winners and also some losers. His next spectacular dream was over ten years later when he dreamed

that a horse called What Man? had won the National at odds of 18–1. But the only horse with a
name comparable to the one he had dreamed of
was a Mr. What?, and the odds were very much
worse, 66–1. So he decided not to touch it. However, on the morning of the race he saw that the
odds had dropped to 18–1. Needless to say, he
backed it and it won, but apparently he has never
been able to "dream predict" since.

A friend of mine recalls having, after the economic measures taken in the U.K. in July 1966, a
series of rather formless but deeply disturbing
dreams about the political and economic future of
the country, suggesting that it would be a generation before there were perceptible improvements.
There was nothing about his personal future in the
dreams, but he consciously changed the direction
of his life from then on so that a few years later he
was able to emigrate with his assets and develop a
more satisfying life. Whether those dreams should
be interpreted as dramatizations of factual evidence
or as some kind of internal vision is a matter of
opinion. The important point is that the subject
believed them to be precognitive and took appropriate action.

Another aspect of dreaming is its time—or
rather timeless—factor. J. W. Dunne equates this
with the concept of each person having two different selves—the first being the everyday one
which lives in the present and the second which is
apart and appears to watch the actions of the first

self. Again this is a common dream phenomenon which most people have experienced when asleep —when they say to themselves, "I know I am dreaming," while watching themselves in the dream. These are often termed "lucid" dreams. I heard an interesting example of one on the radio at the end of January 1983 on the BBC. An American professor dreamed he was talking to a fellow academic whom he disliked. Knowing that he was dreaming he remarked to his colleague, "You realize you are only a figment of my imagination, and to prove that I am too I shall wake myself up." Which he did.

Vision, revelation, trance and dreams can all be precognitive. Dreams are universal, visions not uncommon, revelation and trance much rarer, especially in the foretelling of public events that are the most readily verified; they are the most impressive when validated.

I have avoided in this chapter, or anywhere else in this book, writing about telepathy, vibrations and related matters which seem to me to be best considered as part of the mechanical processes, for want of a better term, by which visions, revelation, trances and dreams come into the mind of a prophet.

As this book is primarily concerned with Nostradamus, it seems appropriate to end this part of it with the description of his own methods of divination, in the first two quatrains of his prophecies, with a translation and explanation.

Estant assisc de nuict secret estude
Seul reposé sur la selle d'aerain;
Flamme exiguë sortant de solitude
Fait propoter qui n'est à croire vaine.

I.1

Sitting alone at night in a secret study;
it is placed on the brass tripod.
A slight flame comes out of the emptiness
and prophesies that which should not be believed
in vain.

In both this and the following quatrain Nostradamus shows that he used the well tried methods of fourth-century neo-Platonist Iamblichus, a reprint of whose book *De Mysteriis Egyptorum* was published in 1547 at Lyons and was certainly read by Nostradamus, as he quotes from it almost verbatim in some of the later predictions. It may well have been the source of his experiments with his earlier essays into prediction in the *Almanacs*.

All the necessary ingredients for magical practices are mentioned in this quatrain. It is night. Nostradamus is sitting alone in his study reading the secret books which inspire him. The use of the brass tripod was a method often used by Iamblichus; on it was placed a bowl of water into which the seer gazed until it became cloudy and visions of the future were revealed. The "flamme exiguë" is almost certainly meant to indicate the inspiration which possessed Nostradamus as, despite himself, he begins to prophesy. It is exactly the same princi-

ple as used with the crystal ball method of divination.

> *La verge en main mise au milieu des*
>   *BRANCHES*
> *De l'onde il moulle et le limbe et le pied:*
> *Un peur et voix fremissant par les manches:*
> *Splendeur divine. Le divin près s'assied.*

I.2

>   *The wand in the hand is placed in the middle of*
> *the legs of the tripod. He sprinkles both the hem of his*
> *garment and his foot with water. A voice: Fear: he trem-*
> *bles in his robes. Divine Splendor. The God sits beside*
> *him.*

In this quatrain Nostradamus continues to explain
his method. Having touched the center of the tripod with his wand, he then moistens his feet and
the edge of his robe with the water that drips from
it. Symbolically this frees him from earthly ties. The
same method was used at the Oracle of Branchus in
Classical times. It seems that Nostradamus fears the
power he evokes. It is important to note that he
hears as well as sees it, and it speaks to him as he
writes down the Prophecies. Once the gift has possessed him, he is not afraid. I feel that this dual
aspect of his prophetic vision is very important to
our interpretation of Nostradamus' gifts, and he
has something in common with the modern American predictor Jeane Dixon, in that his visions appear to more than one sense.

4 NOSTRADAMUS: LIFE AND HISTORY

TO FRANCE AFTER THE DISASTER OF SAINT-QUENTIN

POEM BY RONSARD (1557)

Tu te moques aussi des prophètes que Dieu
Choisit en tes enfants, et les fait au milieu
De ton sein apparaître, afin de te prédire
Ton malheur avenir; mais tu n'en fais que rire:
Ou soit que du grand Dieu l'immense éternité,
Aît de Nostradamus l'enthousiasme excité,
Ou soit que de démon bon ou mauvais l'agite,
Ou soit que de nature il aît l'âme subite,
Et outre les mortels s'élance jusqu'aux cieux,
Et de là nous redit des faits prodigieux;

Ou soit que son esprit sombre et mélancolique,
D'humeurs crasses répu, se rende fantastique;
Bref il est ce qu'il est, si est-ce toutesfois,
Que par les mots douteux de sa prophète voix
Comme un oracle antique, il a de mainte année,
Prédit la plus grande part de nôtre destinée.
Je ne l'eusse pas cru, si le ciel que départ
Bien et mal aux humains, n'eût été de sa part.

TRANSLATION

*You mock also the prophets that God chooses
amongst your children, and places in the midst
of your bosom, in order to predict to you your
future misfortune.*

　　But you only laugh at them.

　　*Perhaps the immense eternity of the great
God has aroused the fervor of Nostradamus.*

　　*Or it has been kindled by a good or bad
demon.*

　　*Or perhaps his spirit is moved by nature,
and soars to the heavens, beyond mortals, and
from there repeats to us prodigious facts.*

　　*Or perhaps his somber and melancholy spirit
is filled with gross humors, making him
fanciful.*

　　*In brief, he is what he is; so it is that always
with the doubtful words of his prophetic voice,
like that of an ancient oracle, he has for many
a year predicted the greater part of our destiny.*

I would not have believed him, had Heaven,
which assigns good and evil to mankind not
been his inspiration.

This sonnet by Ronsard, one of the leading poets
of the mid sixteenth century, shows to some degree
the esteem in which Nostradamus was held during
his own lifetime. His name has become synonymous with that of successful prophecy. The
amount of interest his prophetic works have
aroused since they were printed is quite extraordinary, both in volume and in the wide variations of
meaning alloted to them.

Michel de Nostredame, "the king amongst
prophets" as he has several times been described,
more commonly known by the Latinized form of
his name, Nostradamus, was born on December 14,
1503, by the old Julian calendar (December 23 by
the Gregorian calendar), in St. Rémy de Provence.
His family were not the illustrious line of Jewish-
Italian doctors working at the courts of King René
of Anjou as has been claimed, but people of simple
lineage from around Avignon. His grandfather was
Peyrot or Pierre de Nostredame, an established
grain dealer who married a Gentile girl named
Blanche. Their son, Jaume or Jacques, Nostradamus' father, moved to St. Rémy in 1495 and gave
up the family trade. Here he married Réyniere de
St. Rémy who was the granddaughter of an ex-
doctor turned tax collector.

In an edict of September 26, 1501, Louis XII
gave all Jews the choice of changing to the Catholic

faith within a period of three months and to be baptized, or to leave Provençe. By 1458, at the death of Louis of Aragon, Provençe and Maine had both reverted to the French Crown. The Nostradamus family had definitely been converted by then from Judaism to Catholicism because in 1512, when Nostradamus was nine years old, his parents were listed as being part of the new Christian community. It is important to remember this Jewish element in Nostradamus' background when trying to decipher the Prophecies, as he was certainly influenced by occult Jewish literature. Many biographers claim his family were descended from the tribe of Issachar. Jewish interpreters take this descent to mean the possession of certain skills which included an understanding of the cycles of the sun and the moon, months and feasts and, most importantly, the interpretation of signs from the heavens. Josephus describes the tribe as "knowing the things that were to happen." So whatever other claims have been made regarding Nostradamus' ancestry, this is one that seems to be verified, whether the interpretation was inspired by the publication of the Prophecies or not.

Nostradamus was the eldest son of his family and he probably had four brothers; Bertrand, Hectore, Antoine and Jean. We know almost nothing of the first three but the youngest, Jean, wrote a large number of ribald Provençal songs and commentaries, and eventually became Procureur of the Parlement de Provençe.

Nostradamus' great intellect became apparent

while he was still very young, and his education was put into the hands of his grandfather, Jean, who taught him the rudiments of Latin, Greek, Hebrew, Mathematics and what Nostradamus calls Celestial Science, Astrology. When his grandparent died the boy returned to his parents' house in the rue de Barri and his other grandfather endeavored to continue his education. Soon, however, Nostradamus was sent to Avignon to study, and probably stayed with some of the many cousins he had in the town.

He already showed great interest in astrology and it became common talk among his fellow students, who referred to him as "le petit astrologue." He upheld the Copernican theory that the world was round and circled around the sun more than 100 years before Galileo was prosecuted for the same belief. His parents were quite rightly worried by this attitude because theirs was the age of the Inquisition, and as ex-Jews they were more vulnerable than most. So they sent him off to study medicine at Montpelier in 1522. This university was second only to Paris as a medical school. As early as 1376 it had obtained the then almost "heretical" right from Louis I of Anjou to the body of one convicted criminal a year for dissection. Nostradamus was now nineteen years old and had the advantage of some of the most progressive medical minds in Europe to stimulate him. He obtained his bachelor's degree (baccalauréat) after three years, with apparent ease.

We have many records of the details of this examination. On the actual day the candidate had an oral examination from 8 A.M. until noon, in which his professors tried to catch him out. It was essential that he answered with learning, proof that his studies had given him a maturity equal to theirs. If successful, the student was then officially handed the red robe of the Bachelor of Arts to replace his black student's robe.

To obtain his license to practice medicine, which was not automatic on obtaining his degree, the student then had to deliver five lectures over a period of three months, the subjects of which were chosen by the Dean of the University. These were followed by further "per intentionem" exams in which the candidate was given four questions to answer, each handed to him a day in advance, and each of which had to be discoursed upon for an hour, in Latin of course, before a different professor. This lasted for one or two days. Eight days later the candidate was given a fifth question to answer, without any research, by the Chancellor of the University himself. If he survived this, he then had to write a thesis on some aphorism of Hippocrates by the following day. These last two tests were so severe and stressful they were known as "les points rigoreux." When one thinks of modern day finals at university the sheer length of time it took to become qualified appears quite staggering. But since I will be dealing later on in the book in more detail with the great importance placed by both the medievals and occultists on the now almost lost "art of memory," let me just repeat that it was a prodigious feat by any standards, particularly when one realizes that this only comprised the last part of the students' doctorate. However, Nostradamus got his baccalauréat and was given his license to practice medicine by the Bishop of Montpelier in 1525.

Plague was endemic in Southern France during the sixteenth century, in particular a very virulent form known locally as "le charbon" because of the great black pustules that appeared on the body of the victim. Nostradamus had many detractors throughout his lifetime but not one has ever denied his courage in facing disease, his humanity, his kindness toward the sick, and his generosity toward the poor. It was at this early stage, 1525, that his reputation as a healer started to become known. He traveled the countryside, arriving at Narbonne where he stayed for a while, possibly in order to study with the well-known School of Jewish/crypto-Christian alchemists who flourished there. He continued traveling to various stricken towns dispensing his own cures, the prescriptions for which are found in a book, *Le Traité des fardemens*, published in 1552. He is reputed to have scorned the traditional protective "magical" robe of the plague doctor, made of materials of seven colors, which English doctors were still using a hundred years later at the time of the Great Plague of London. He was, however, very unsettled and eventually went to Carcassonne where he worked for a while in the household of the Bishop Amenien de Fays, for whom he prescribed his famous elixir of life and virility which was also included in the 1552 book, *Le Traité*.

We next hear of him at Toulouse in the rue de la Triperie, again at Bordeaux where the plague was severe and then back at Avignon where he remained studying for some months. His interest in magic and the occult may spring from this period of his life, for the library at Avignon held many occult books. At the same time he managed to concoct a delicious recipe for quince jelly for the Papal Legate and the Grand Master of the Knights of Malta who were then in the town. It is a good recipe but with rather too much sugar for modern tastes. One must remember that sugar was very expensive at this time, and to use it lavishly in cooking was an indication of wealth and status.

After nearly four years of sporadic traveling he returned to Montpelier to complete his doctorate and re-enrolled on October 23, 1529.

The next series of examinations he had to pass were known as Les Triduanes. For these the candidate had to prepare a list of twelve subjects on which he might be examined. Six of these were then chosen, three by lot, and three by the Dean. Then the candidate had to argue his case. We are told that Nostradamus was hard pressed to explain his more unorthodox remedies and treatments, and that his success and renown had preceded him, making him enemies among the faculty. But his learning and ability could not be denied and he

obtained his doctorate which entitled him to wear
the distinctive square cap, the same as the one we
see in his portrait in the Church of Salon, and the
gold ring of the healer, together with the presenta-
tion of a copy of Hippocrates' works. When offered
a job on the faculty Nostradamus remained there
teaching for approximately one year, but by this
time his theories, such as his refusal to bleed patients, and his own restless nature caused him to set
off on his wanderings again, probably sometime in
1532. He was always to suffer from this wanderlust,
and in his dark cape and cap, he must have appeared the epitome of the Wandering Jew. It is
interesting to note that Rabelais received his degree
at Montpelier in 1530, but there is no indication
that the two men ever met.

Nostradamus traveled for the next two years
passing through Bordeaux, La Rochelle and
Toulouse. While practicing there he received a letter from Julius César Scaliger, the philosopher considered second only to Erasmus in Europe and
whose Renaissance interests included medicine, poetry, philosophy, botany and mathematics. Apparently Nostradamus' reply so pleased Scaliger that
he invited him to stay at his home in Agen. This life
suited Nostradamus admirably, and circa 1534 he
married a young girl "of high estate, very beautiful
and admirable," whose name unfortunately has not
come down to us. He had a son and a daughter by
her and his life seemed complete. His practice was
famous and profitable and he had the brilliant

mind of Scaliger and those of the many visitors and travelers who came to see them to sharpen his wits and broaden his intellectual horizons.

Then, in approximately 1537, a series of tragedies struck. The plague came to Agen and, despite all his efforts, killed Nostradamus' wife and two children. The fact that he was unable to save his own family had a disastrous effect on his practice. Then he quarreled with Scaliger and lost his friendship—a not unlikely happening, as Scaliger quarreled with all his friends sooner or later. To Nostradamus' credit he did not return the abuse. He still refers to Scaliger in the *Traité des fardemens* as one "who has inherited Cicero's soul in the matter of eloquence, Virgil's in poetry and Galen's at least twice in medicine. I owe him more than any other person in the world." A very magnanimous tribute. His late wife's family tried to sue him for the return of her dowry and as the final straw, in 1538, he was accused of heresy because of a chance remark made some years before, which had been reported to the authorities. To a workman casting a bronze statue of the Virgin, Nostradamus had commented that he was making devils. His plea that he was only describing the lack of aesthetic appeal inherent in the statue was ignored and the Inquisitors sent for him to go to Toulouse. Nostradamus, naturally having no wish to stand trial nor to suffer the rack or the stake, immediately set out on his wanderings again, keeping well clear of the Church authorities for the next six years.

Nostradamus did not marry again until 1547, when he settled down with a comfortably-off widow of Salon-en-Provence, by whom he had six children. The most prolific, César de Nostradamus, was only nineteen when his father died but did much to keep the stories of his father alive in his eventual, monumental tome, *Histoire de Provence.*

Little is known of his route except for odd references he lets drop in a later work, *Moultes Opuscules.* He seems to have been in Lorraine, Venice and Sicily, collecting material for his book in the way of recipes, prescriptions for medicines and, one must presuppose, visits to the important astrologers, alchemists and kabalists.

It was probably around this period that he started to translate the *Horus Apollo* of Philippus from the Greek into French. It is nothing but a collection of treatises on ethics and philosophy and is of no great literary merit. Legends about Nostradamus' prophetic powers also start to appear at this time. Apparently when in Italy he saw a young monk who had been a swineherd pass by him in the street, and immediately knelt down in the mud and called him "Your Holiness." Felice Peretti became Sixtus V in 1585, long after Nostradamus' death.

There is another amusing tale concerning a certain Seigneur de Florinville, who was discoursing with Nostradamus about prophecy and asked him to put his gift to the test by telling him the fates of the two suckling pigs in his yard. Nostradamus replied that the Seigneur would eat the black pig and a wolf the white one. Immediately de Florinville went to his cook and ordered the white pig to be killed for that night's dinner, which it duly was. Unfortunately a tame wolf-cub belonging to the lord's men stole the meat. The terrified cook killed the black pig and served it for dinner. Seigneur de Florinville then told Nostradamus that they were now eating the white pig. When Nostradamus insisted that it was the black one, the cook was sent for and confessed to the whole incident.

There is a legend that he spent some time in the Cistercian Abbey of Orval in the Belgian commune of Villiers devant Orval. In the early nineteenth century two faked prose prophecies predicting the advent of Napoleon were discovered. One, the *Prophecy of Philip Olivarius,* dated 1542, was probably printed about 1810. This is the book which, according to Mlle. Le Normand, Napoleon's prophetic advisor and friend, the Emperor was reputed to carry around with him all the time. The second book was called *The Prophecy of Orval,* dated 1544, and was probably actually produced around 1839. Several of the great Nostradamus commentators, including Barreste (c. 1840) and the Abbé Torné Chavigny (1862–1878) were convinced that they were written by Nostradamus. They are unlikely even to be copies of Nostradamus' earlier lost work for stylistic reasons alone—and again, Nostradamus' stay at Orval exists only in oral history, possibly one of the many examples of the abuse of his prophetic powers.

By 1554 Nostradamus had settled in Marseilles

together with Louis Serres. In November of that
year Provençe experienced one of the worst floods
in its history. This period is well chronicled by
Nostradamus' son, César, in his *Histoire de Provençe*.
The plague redoubled in virulence, spread by the
waters and the polluted corpses. Nostradamus
worked ceaselessly. Most doctors had fled with
those people who were still well enough to move,
thus carrying the infection farther. According to
contemporary memoirs, the plague was particularly bad at Aix, the capital of Provençe, and the
city sent for Nostradamus on May 1. He was alone
throughout the epidemic, working among the sick,
curing many, and insisting on fresh air and un-
polluted water. The sense of hopelessness was so
great when he first arrived in the city that he saw
one sick woman sewing herself into her own shroud
because she knew there would be no one to do it for
her when she was dead. Nostradamus writes of his
work here in great detail. In fact, chapter VIII of
the *Moultes Opuscules* contains nothing but descriptions of his time at Aix. He gives a formula for the
famous rose pills he used as a protection against the
plague. The ingredients were as follows:

> *1 oz. sawdust from the green cyprus*
> *6 oz. Iris of Florence*
> *3 oz. cloves*
> *3 drams sweet smelling calamus*
> *6 drams lign aloes*
> *3/400 roses*

The method of preparation was complicated to

say the least. The roses had to be picked before dawn, pulverized and mixed with a powder made from the remaining ingredients. They must not be exposed to air. The mixture was then made into pills which the patient had to suck at all times. Nostradamus claimed that their magnificent scent killed bad breath and smells, and cleaned decaying teeth, a very common problem at that period.

Presumably Nostradamus assumed that the purified air kept the patient clear of the plague. Modern science knows better, that plague, particularly the kind endemic in Southern France, i.e., "le charbon," with the characteristic black pustules on the body, is transmitted by fleas leaving infected rats. Despite this, Nostradamus' success as a plague doctor went unchallenged. The City Parliament at Aix voted him a lifetime pension when the plague abated.

Once the city recovered, Nostradamus moved on to Salon, which he found so pleasant a town that he determined to settle there for the rest of his life. But almost immediately the city of Lyons sent for him to cure a pestilence which may, in fact, have been an epidemic of whooping cough. Whatever it was, once over, Nostradamus returned home laden with yet more gifts from the grateful citizens. Characteristically, he gave many away to the poor of the town before leaving. It is difficult to separate truth from legend in these reports of his great generosity but they are so frequent that they almost certainly have some foundation in fact.

He returned home to Salon and the following

November he married one Ann Ponsart Gemelle, a rich local widow. Their marriage contract still exists in the Salon archives, dated November 11, 1547 and signed by Master Etienne Hozier, the notary of Salon. The house in which he spent the remainder of his days still stands off the Place de la Poissonnerie. He seems to have settled down to a quieter life, spending most of his time making special cosmetic preparations for the local gentry by whom he was eagerly received. He does not seem to have practiced much medicine at this period. He was, however, unpopular with many of the local peasantry, the Cabans, whose religious fervor, mixed no doubt with jealousy, often led them to look askance at the wealthier Huguenot families. It is most unlikely that Nostradamus was a Huguenot sympathizer, but during the later days of the religious troubles he was certainly a target for the Cabans' hostility.

His interest in the occult was strong and presumably he was still experiencing odd flashes of prophetic insight, because by 1550 he published his first *Almanac*. This was a simple series of verses describing the weather, crops, local conditions and suchlike. It was so successful that he published one almost every year until his death. "They were so well regarded," wrote M. La Croix du Maine in 1594, "and sold so well that several imitations of them were made under his name, composed by ignorant people full of lies." Perhaps it was this success that encouraged him to undertake the much more onerous task of writing the Prophecies.

It was also around this period that another of
Nostradamus' interests, equally as enduring as his
Prophecies, became apparent. He became the pa-
tron of a local architect and engineer, Adam de la
Craponne, who intended to construct a canal between the Rhône and the Durance rivers, thus
turning the arid fields around Salon into a fertile
plain. Nostradamus not only contributed large
sums of money to the project—which still functions
to this day—but apparently also gave encourage-
ment and advice.

Nostradamus converted the top room of his
house at Salon into a study and as he tells us in the
Prophecies, worked there at night with his occult
books. He also mentions later that he burned many
of them once he had finished with them, but it is
difficult to believe that a true scholar could possibly
do this. It was more probably an attempt to mislead
the Church authorities. The main source of his
magical inspirations was a book called *De Mysteriis
Egyptorum,* a copy of which was published at Lyons
in 1547, and which Nostradamus almost certainly
possessed, as I have already mentioned.

Sometime in 1554, a certain Jean-Aymes de
Chavigny, a former mayor of Beaune, gave up his
position in that city and came to Nostradamus as a
pupil, in order to study judicial astrology and astronomy. He was aged 30, a doctor of theology and
law and had been supposed to have a brilliant future ahead of him. But he sacrificed it all in the
further pursuit of knowledge. The spur for this
action probably came from the Court poet, Jean

Dorat, who professed to Chavigny a great admiration for Nostradamus' works. Dorat's was no lightweight mind; as well as his Court post he held the position of Professor of Greek at the Collège de France. Chavigny wrote several books about Nostradamus after the prophet's death and he certainly helped edit the first complete edition of the *Prophecies* of 1568. However, like Nostradamus' son César, he seems to have exaggerated his importance with regard to the prophet. The evidence for this lies in Nostradamus' will, a long and detailed document referring not only to his money but specifying all his possessions.

There is no reference to Chavigny in it, nor in Nostradamus' papers which he states specifically are to be left to whichever of his sons, on reaching maturity, "has drunk the smoke of the lamp," i.e., is a true scholar. It is not known which son eventually acquired these papers. Chavigny did however edit a great many of them, probably with the consent of Nostradamus' widow.

His will was drawn up on July 17, 1566, by the local notary, Joseph Roche. Nostradamus specified the various monies he possessed, which came to about 3,444 crowns. Of his six children, his daughter Madeleine received the largest legacy of 600 crowns, her two sisters Anne and Diana each getting only 500. The three sons received 100 crowns each on their twenty-fifth birthdays. He left various bequests to religious orders and six sous to the thirteen beggars in the town. He even included instructions as to his burial. But family bickering must have gone on behind his back and three days later he added to the codicil which gave César his astrolobe and a large golden ring, and Madeleine was given two walnut coffers, with all the clothes, jewelry and whatever else they contained, before her marriage.

To revert to the success of the *Almanacs:* Nostradamus was continuing with his other writings, prescriptions for illness and cosmetics, recipes for preserves, and finally the publication of the *Horus Apollo.* His famous *Traité des fardemens* finally appeared in 1552.

By 1554 Nostradamus' view was that a crucial period was due in European affairs. According to his son César in his *Histoire de Provençe,* several omens seemed to reinforce this opinion.

"In the year 1554 sad and unhappy events began, and fellow beings appeared both hideously deformed and prodigious. January had just ended when a monstrous child with two heads was born at Sénas which one couldn't look at without a feeling of revulsion. He had been predicted some time previously by people with foreknowledge of future happenings. Apparently this wretched deformity was taken to be shown to Nostradamus, and this, combined with the birth of a two-headed horse near Salon about six weeks later, caused Nostradamus to prophesy a deep rift in France's future." In view of the religious troubles at the time this did not require great perspicacity. France was to suffer four civil wars before the ascent to the throne by Henri de Navarre, signaling the end of the royal line of the Valois kings.

I myself saw a stuffed black lamb with two heads in 1976. The old lady to whom it belonged remembered its birth on their Berkshire farm and its running around the fields with the other lambs for about a week until it died. Her father, a farmer, grew very upset by the interest it aroused and the portents of bad luck that were expressed by neighbors—and this was in the first decade of this century!

These ugly omens must have appeared while Nostradamus was in the middle of writing the *Prophecies*—his book of predictions as he conceived them would cover time until the end of the world. Chavigny wrote of them in 1594:

> *He [Nostradamus] set himself to write his Centuries which he kept for a long time before publishing them, because he felt that the strangeness of the content could not fail to cause detractions, calumnies and extremely venomous accusations, which indeed happened. But finally, overcome by his desire to be of service to the public, he revealed them, with the result that their fame and renown ran without check through the mouths of both French and foreigners alike with the greatest interest and wonder.*

In 1555, the first part of the *Prophecies* was duly finished and published at Lyons in an incomplete form. It contained the First Preface dedicated to his son César, Centuries I to III in their entirety and 53 quatrains of Century IV. By 1557 the rest of the first part up to the still incomplete Century VII was also in print. The word Century has nothing to do with one hundred years: the verses were so called because they were grouped into a series of one hundred quatrains, of which Nostradamus intended to write ten, making one thousand quatrains in all. For some unknown reason, the Seventh Century was never completed, and there are indications among his papers that Nostradamus was considering adding an Eleventh and Twelfth Century, which was prevented by his death.

The verses are written in a crabbed, obscure style, in a polyglot vocabulary of French, Provençal, Italian, Greek and Latin. In order to avoid being prosecuted as a magician, Nostradamus writes that he deliberately confused the time sequence of the Prophecies so that their secrets would not be revealed to the noninitiate. It is extraordinary how quickly the fame of Nostradamus spread across France and Europe on the strength of the *Prophecies*. At this time books were an expensive luxury and were usually owned and read only by the rich, for most of the population was illiterate. The *Prophecies* became all the rage at Court, but despite their popularity many educated people reviled them, particularly doctors and astrologers who accused Nostradamus of disgracing his professional status. A clever Latinized pun upon his name was soon circulating throughout France:

Nostradamus cum falsa damus, nam fallere
nostrum est:
Et cum falsa damus, nil nisi nostra damus.

This roughly translates into English, but without the punning as—"We give that which is our own when we give something false, for it is in our nature to be false. And when we give false things, they are nothing but our own."

Some of the Prophecies seemed to invoke a certain uneasiness among the courtiers, particularly one which appeared to predict the death in a duel of Henry II, King of France. Be that as it may, the Queen Catherine de Medici sent for Nostradamus to come to Court by Royal Command, and he set out for Paris on July 14, 1556. The journey took only one month instead of the more usual eight weeks because the Queen had horses posted for him. On August 15, Nostradamus booked a room at the Inn of St. Michel, a good augury perhaps, near Notre Dame. The Queen must have been very anxious to see him because she sent for him the next day and the Chief Constable took him to the Court at St. Germain en Laye.

One could only wish that there had been a witness to record their meeting. Nostradamus and the Queen spoke together for about two hours. It is said that one of the reasons Catherine sent for Nostradamus was quatrain 35 of Century I. It was remarkably similar to a prediction that had been made earlier in February of that year, 1556, by Luc

Gauric, the famous Italian astrologer. He had written to Henri II, Catherine's husband, warning him to avoid all single combat in enclosed spaces particularly around his forty-first year, for about that time he could be threatened with a wound in the head, blindness and possibly death. The contents of this letter were certainly known to the Court. The King is recorded as discussing it with Anne de Montmorency, the Constable of France, and two courtiers, Claude d'Aubespine and Brantôme, refer to it in their memoirs. Nostradamus' prediction ran as follows:

> *Le lion jeune le vieux surmontera,*
> *En champ bellique par singulier duelle:*
> *Dans caige d'or les yeux lui crevera,*
> *Deux classes une, puis mourir, mort cruelle.*
>
> *I.35*

The young lion will overcome the older one, in a field of combat in single fight: He will pierce his eyes in their golden cage; two wounds in one, then he dies a cruel death.

Catherine is reputed to have asked him about the quatrain concerning the king's death and to have been satisfied with his answer. Certainly she continued to believe Nostradamus' predictions until her death. The king, Henri II, granted Nostradamus only a brief audience and was not greatly interested, although he sent him one hundred golden crowns, and Catherine sent another thirty. This seemed poor recompense to Nostradamus, who had expended one hundred crowns for his journey alone. He was forced to borrow money from a certain M. Morel on his arrival in Paris. This fact is mainly of interest because the only known extant letter signed by Nostradamus is written to Morel (ms. 8589 Bib. Nat.) in which he acknowledges receiving a letter from the latter in November 1561, sent by Morel from Paris on October 12. The letter states that when Nostradamus was in trouble in Paris in 1556 (his visit to Catherine de Medici), Morel lent him two rose nobles and twelve crowns. Nostradamus had mentioned it to the Queen, assuming as was customary, that she would pay his debts, but she did not attend to them. This letter from Morel was a second reminder, and in reply, Nostradamus says that he never received the first one. He answers very courteously and apparently enclosed two notes of credit to friends at Court who would repay Morel. He adds that he hopes to visit Paris soon, when the religious troubles calm down, to see about the education of his son César, and that he would very much like to see Morel then. The letter is first signed by a secretary, probably Chavigny, followed by Nostradamus' own signature.

However, his lodgings were soon exchanged for the grandeur of the palace of the Archbishop of Sens, where he remained for some two weeks. The Queen then sent for him a second time and now Nostradamus was faced with the delicate and difficult task of drawing up the horoscopes of seven surviving Valois children, whose tragic fates he had already revealed in the Centuries. All he would tell Catherine was that all her sons would be kings, which is slightly inaccurate since one of them, François, died before he could inherit. If on the other hand what he actually said was that he saw four kings to come, then the prediction was accurate because Henri III was king of Poland before returning to be king of France.

Many tales of prophetic warnings and help abound about this period. Nostradamus apparently suffered one of his periodic attacks of gout and was confined to his lodgings. He had spent much of this time telling the futures of many of the richer citizens who flocked to have their horoscopes drawn up. He was resting when suddenly there was a violent knocking on the door of his room. The noble Beauvais family had lost a valuable dog and had sent a page to ask Nostradamus where they should search. But before the boy could say anything and without opening the door, Nostradamus called out that he should go and look for the dog on the road to Orléans, where it would be found, on a leash. When he went there the page met a servant leading the dog home. The story spread like wildfire around the Court and city, and Nostradamus' reputation grew accordingly.

Soon afterward Nostradamus was warned that the Justices of Paris were inquiring about his magic practices, and he returned quickly to Salon. He was welcomed home as a person of importance. From this time on, suffering from gout and arthritis, he seems to have done little except draw up horoscopes for his many distinguished visitors and complete the writing of the *Prophecies*. Apparently he allowed a few manuscript copies to circulate before publication because many of the predictions were understood and quoted before the completed book came off the printing press in toto, in 1568, two years after his death. This was common practice.

The reason for this reticence was probably the death of the king which occurred in 1559. Nostradamus had predicted it in I.35 and may have felt that it was too explicit for comfort and that it would be advisable to wait a few years before publishing the *Prophecies* in full.

In the summer of 1559 the French royal house celebrated two very important weddings, both politically valuable to the stability of the Valois line. Henri and Catherine's daughter and the king's sister were married in a splendid double celebration, Elizabeth, by proxy, to Philip II of Spain, and Marguerite, the king's sister, to the Duke of Savoy. Following this, three days of festivities and celebrations had been planned, the culmination of which was a series of tournaments to be held in the rue Saint Antoine. For the first two days the king was victorious in all his jousts. On the third day he rode against Gabriel Lorges, Comte de Montgomery, who was Captain of the Scottish Guard. Montgomery got a touch, but failed to unseat the king, who demanded another bout. In the third charge, Montgomery's lance splintered against the king's lance but it was dropped too late. The point broke through the golden visor of the king's helmet and pierced him in the eye. It took him ten days to die, in appalling agony. It is recounted that Catherine had an appalling premonition before this final joust and sent a note to the king begging him to desist. Montgomery is also on record as stating that he did not want to continue and an anonymous small boy amongst the spectators cried that the king must not fight. On being questioned afterward, he could give no explanation for his fears. But the king would listen to none of them, with the subsequent result.

Montgomery wisely fled the Court, despite Henri's demand that he should be treated with clemency. Rightly so, for Catherine never forgave him and, as predicted in the *Prophecies,* she eventually caught up with him and imprisoned him. Montmorency, the Constable of France, is reputed to have said "Cursed be the divine who predicted it, so evilly and so well." It is not certain whether he was referring to Luc Gauric or Nostradamus, but the public was sure it was the latter, and Nostradamus was burned in effigy in a Paris square. There were also demands that the Church should deal with him—shades of the Inquisition of Toulouse two decades earlier.

Nostradamus remained safely in Salon protected by the favor of the now Queen Regent and Francis

II who succeeded his father Henri. But any hope of continuing obscurity was dashed in November 1560, when the young king fell into some type of coma. He was married to Mary, Queen of Scots, whose childhood had been spent with her mother Mary de Guise at the French Court after the death of her father, James V of Scotland. By mid-month Michel Suriano, the Venetian ambassador, wrote to the Doge from Orléans. (The manuscript, in copied form, can be found in the Bibliothèque Nationale.) It states; "Each courtier recalls now the 39th quatrain of Century X of Nostradamus and comments upon it under his breath." It goes as follows:

> *Premier fils veufve malheureux mariage,*
> *Sans nuls enfans deux Isles en discorde,*
> *Avant dixhuict incompetant eage,*
> *De l'autre pres plus bas sera l'accord.*

X.39

> *The first son, a widow, an unfortunate marriage without any children: two Islands thrown into discord. Before eighteen years of age, a minor: of the other even earlier will be the betrothal.*

This clearly describes the betrothal of Francis II to Mary Stuart, an unfortunate marriage which was childless. Because of Mary's return to Scotland she caused discord between England and her own country. Francis was still not quite eighteen years old when he died (seventeen years, ten months, fifteen days). His younger brother Charles IX was betrothed to Elizabeth of Austria when only eleven years old.

By the beginning of December, Niccolo Tornabuoni, the Ambassador of Tuscany, wrote in these terms to Duke Cosimo of Florence. "The health of the king is uncertain and Nostradamus, in his predictions for this month, says that the royal house will lose two young members from an unforeseen malady." Francis II died on December 5 and the young heir of the junior branch of the Valois family of Roche-sur-Yon also died within the month.

By now Nostradamus' reputation was widely bruited abroad. In January 1561, the Spanish ambassador, Chantonnay, wrote to his king, Philip II. "People have noticed that in one month the first and last members of the Royal House have died. These catastrophes have struck the Court into a stupor, together with the warning of Nostradamus, whom it would be better to chastize than allow to sell his prophecies, which lead to vain and superstitious beliefs." Suriano wrote again to the Doge in May. "There is another prediction widely spread in France, coming from the writings of this famous divine astrologer, Nostradamus, which threatens all three brothers, saying that the Queen Mother will see them all as kings." (Archives Nationales K.1494).

It was around this time that Nostradamus received a letter from the Bishop of Orange asking for help in tracing a silver chalice that had been stolen. The prophet's reply, still in the Arles archives, starts with a horoscope which he does not elaborate upon. He then goes on to say that Orange would suffer a dreadful pestilence if the chalice were not returned immediately, and that the thief would die an appalling death. He continues by advising the Bishop to post the letter in a public place. But unfortunately we have no record as to whether this method produced any results.

Another apocryphal story which best indicated the general reputation surrounding Nostradamus at this time is related here. The prophet was sitting in the evening by the door of his house when the daughter of a friend went by on her way to the woods. The dialogue is reputed to have gone somewhat as follows:

> *"Bonjour M. de Nostredame."*
> *"Bonjour fillette." (young girl)*

On her return she spoke to him again to receive the answer,

> *"Bonjour petite femme." (young woman)*

Nostradamus seems to have known what the young girl was up to in the woods and that she had lost her virginity that evening.

In the autumn of 1559, the Duke of Savoy, who had married Henri II's daughter at the time of the tragic celebrations which resulted in the king's death earlier in the year, passed through Salon on the way to Nice. While there he learned that the plague was widespread in his kingdom and decided to remain in the small Provençal town. His wife, Marguerite, joined him toward the end of the year and all Salon turned out to welcome her with the traditional arches and inscriptions. According to César Nostradamus, "the Princess entertained the elder Nostradamus for a long time and did him much honor." His connections with lesser French royalty continued. In 1561 the Duke and his wife asked Nostradamus for the horoscope of their yet unborn son, who was to be Charles-Emmanuel. Nostradamus was rather off the track when he declared that he would become the greatest captain of his age. But at least he correctly predicted a boy, and he could certainly offer in his own defense the fact that he had neither the hour or place of birth, essential for an exact horoscope. But Charles-Emmanuel was known as the Great, and was a persistent thorn in the flesh of Henri IV, so the prophet was partially vindicated.

In 1564, Catherine, the Queen Regent, decided to make a Royal Progress through France with her second son, Charles IX, and the rest of her family, in a desperate attempt to pacify the various religious factions. The progress was to take two years and end up at the Spanish border where she would see her daughter Elizabeth and Philip II. She "reduced" the court entourage to a minimum of 800 followers. When traveling through Provençe it was natural enough that the royal party should stop at Salon and see Nostradamus. They arrived at 3 P.M. on October 17. A few days earlier plague had suddenly broken out in the town and many people had left, so that the triumphal arches and decorations for the royal route left something to be desired. The king was so incensed he ordered that everyone should return under pain of heavy penalties.

The streets had been covered with sand and strewn with branches of rosemary. The king rode an African horse with gray trappings, the harness was of black velvet and trimmed with gold fringes. He wore a cloak of Tyrian purple with silver borders and ribbons and large amethyst earrings. Nostradamus, uncharacteristically, one feels, refused to greet the noble guests at their official welcome, but waited until the king asked to speak to him. César describes Nostradamus as going up to the château carrying a velvet hat in one hand and a Malacca cane with a silver handle in the other, because by this time his gout had became very troublesome. The Queen Regent insisted on seeing all his family "even down to a little baby girl in arms," probably his sixth child, Diana. She then asked him to draw up the horoscope of Edward of Anjou, who as Henry III would be the last Valois king. Catherine was satisfied with the reply that her youngest son would come to power. Little did she know that in her entourage was a page who would install a new bloodline on the French throne—the future Henri IV of Navarre. But Nostradamus was well aware of it. He had noticed the boy in the royal entourage and wanted to see him naked; divination by the position of moles on the body was very com-

mon at this time. However, the young Henri took
fright and fled, so Nostradamus arranged that he
should be present at his levée the following morning, and observed him as he went naked through
various rituals before being handed his shirt. He
then declared the young prince would eventually
inherit the kingdom of France.

When the royal party left Salon they went via
various towns to Arles. Charles IX then sent for the
prophet with a gift of 200 gold crowns to which the
queen added another hundred and created him her
Court Physician in Ordinary. This carried with it
various favors, including a salary and status, which
doubtless pleased Nostradamus very much.

This visit provides an interesting sidelight into
the actual course of English history, preserved by
the new Spanish ambassador to the French Court,
Don Francisco de Alva, who liked Nostradamus as
little as had his predecessor Chantonnay. One of
his letters of this period to Philip II states: "Tomorrow there leaves secretly a gentleman sent to
the Queen of England." (It is believed this was
Throckmorton, the British ambassador at that
time.) "I know that the ambassador is jealous. The
first day that the King and Queen saw Nostradamus he declared that the king would marry the
English Queen" (Elizabeth I). Elizabeth's tactfully
recorded reply to this embassy was "Charles IX is
too great and too small to become my husband."
An unsuccessful prediction, but it was soon followed by Nostradamus' suggestion that it should be

the Duc d'Anjou (later Henri III) who should go and seek the hand of the much older virgin queen. She christened him "The Frog" and he spent an ambiguous year in the English Court before returning home. However, he was useful to Elizabeth, as she was able to play her usual political games and balance one suitor against another without commitment.

One feels that old age, illness and political pressures were becoming too much for the prophet. Another prediction made by him which also turned out to be completely erroneous was fervently accepted by the Queen. In a letter written to Montmorency from Salon, Catherine states that Nostradamus "promises a fine future for the king, my son, and that he will live as long as you, whom he says will see 90 years before dying." No wonder Throckmorton told Elizabeth that Catherine quoted the prophet "with as confident an air as she had quoted St. John or St. Luke." Ironically, Montmorency died aged seventy-four in 1567, to be followed by the King, Charles IX, aged twenty-four, in 1574.

For the last two years of his life royal patronage ensured Nostradamus a life of favors and honor. But he was crippled with arthritis and gout. It is interesting that among all the prophets of whom one reads, including those discussed in this book, Nostradamus was one of the very few who made a financial profit out of his gift. Most people able to predict the future, Edgar Cayce is a good modern example, never manage to accrue money, to the great distress of their families and dependents. They seemed to believe that to do so would diminish their powers. Clearly, Nostradamus had no such doubts.

Toward the end of June Nostradamus was suffering from severe dropsy, and being a doctor, he realized that his death was near. He sent for the local Franciscan friar on July 1, to hear his confession and administer the last sacraments. When Chavigny came to say good night to him, Nostradamus informed him that he would not be alive at sunrise. He was found, as he himself had predicted, lying on a bench, which had been used as an aid to help his swollen, tortured body climb up into his bed; "trouvé tout mort entre le lit et le banc."

5 PAST EVIDENCE: UP TO 1945

If any credence is to be given to a particular prophet and his predictions, they must be clearly proven to be genuine and preferably to have appeared in print during his lifetime, and be seen to be fulfilled since the prophet's death. Oral legend is too vague and subject to too many distortions. But it is also essential that the reader understand the "philosophy of prediction" if one may term it that. The function of a prophet is to give warning of possible future disaster. It does not preclude the option of free will, and its message is: do what is necessary, in time, or this particular situation may happen. Man is a free agent; he must therefore sum up each individual set of circumstances and use his option to act. Since prophets are, almost without exception, excellent purveyors of doom and gloom, man must always be aware that a prediction records only one possible side of the coin. Man can change the future should he so wish. When this happens the prophet may well appear to be proven wrong. All, including Nostradamus, have obviously written erroneous predictions, but it is impossible to know whether these are genuine mistakes in the interpretation of astrological data or whatever, or the result of a man's deliberate action, choosing to alter the possible future. A good example of this is the quatrain which Ernst Krafft interpreted as meaning Hitler was in danger (VI.51). Had he not done so, Hitler might well have been killed, the Second World War would never have happened and possibly Nostradamus' Second Anti-Christ would never have come to power. It is a sobering thought.

It may well be possible for an intelligent person to divine what might happen in the near future. In fact, in the short term, I think it certainly is possible. But when people such as Nostradamus, who is exceptional at this, provide us with a wealth of proper names, dates, places and events ranging over four centuries, usually specifically interlinked, it takes more than the average skepticism to deny that he certainly had some sort of prophetic gift.

Like all prophets, Nostradamus has his limitations. He cannot always understand the content of the vision he sees, or finds it almost impossible to explain in his sixteenth-century vocabulary. The necessary words just did not exist. Thus, in V.8 he attempts to describe bombs in the following terms:

> *Sera laissé le feu vif, mort caché*
> *Dedans les globes horrible espouvantable . . .*

> *There will be let loose living fire and hidden death,*
> *fearful inside dreadful globes . . .*

V.8

Rockets seem to be described as machines of flying fire.

> *Du feu volant la machination . . .*

VI.34

Submarines become iron fish enclosing men, usually traveling with a warlike intent.

> *Qu'en dans poisson fer et lettres enfermée*
> *Hors sortira qui puis fera la guerre.*

II.5

When documents are enclosed in the iron fish, out of it will come a man who will then make war. In IV.43 he envisages weapons heard fighting in the skies.

> *Seront ouis au ciel les armes battre . . .*

IV.43

All these ideas are reasonably clear to twentieth-century interpreters, but they were not so to Nostradamus' contemporaries. His grasp of the concept of flying machines, airplanes, is particularly vivid, as is, also, their possible use in a warlike situation.

Les fleurs* passés diminue le monde,
Long temps la paix terres inhabitées;
Seul marchera par ciel, terre, mer et onde,
Puis de nouveau les guerres suscitées.

I.63

Pestilences extinguished, the world becomes smaller, for a long time the lands will be peacefully inhabited. People will travel safely through the sky, [over] land and sea; then wars will start up again.

The most interesting aspect of this quatrain is the manner in which Nostradamus grasps the very twentieth-century concept that air travel makes the whole world accessible—it "becomes smaller." It is worth noting that the so-called era of world peace since 1945 is the longest unbroken one this century. But it is soon to be broken if we are to believe Nostradamus. The extinguished pestilence may refer to disease or the after-effects of the Second World War. Nostradamus also has an uncanny comprehension of pilots needing oxygen when flying and their use of radio to communicate. If one bears these two facts in mind, plus the limitations imposed by his vocabulary and chosen verse form, the next quatrain, I.64, becomes readily intelligible.

De nuict soleil penseront avoir veu
Quant le pourceau demi-homme on verra;
Bruict, chant, bataille au ciel battre aperceu;
Et bestes brutes à parler lon orra.

I.64

---

*Fleurs—read fléaux; plague, pestilence.

At night they will think they have seen the sun,
when they see the man who is half-pig. Noise, screams,
battles seen fought in the skies. The brute beasts will be
heard to speak.

Nostradamus describes a vivid picture of a battle
in the air—the sun being exploding bombs or perhaps a searchlight piercing the sky. The piglike
man, which no commentator had deciphered before my book of 1973, *The Prophecies of
Nostradamus,** seems a clear picture of a pilot in sil-
houette wearing an oxygen mask, helmet and gog-
gles. The oxygen breathing apparatus does look
remarkably like a pig's snout. The battle is clearly
described as being fought in the air; the screams
may be the sound of dropping bombs as they whine
to earth. The battle is clearly watched, "aperçu," by
people on the ground. It is important to understand the wording of the last line. The aeroplanes,
"bestes brutes," are heard talking to others. Could
this be a forecast of radio communication? Certainly this quatrain helps to convince me that
Nostradamus' visions were of two dimensions, both
visual and aural.

He also uses a special vocabulary to help distinguish the time element in the quatrains. These
"trigger words" are of immense importance when
trying to unravel his secrets. A good example of
this is the way that until the advent of Napoleon,

*The Prophecies of Nostradamus. Translated, edited and interpreted by Erika
Cheetham. New updated and revised edition. Corgi/Transworld, 1981.

France is referred to as a kingdom. After that it is an Empire, with an Emperor. There are many similar examples. But when any prophet quotes dates which occur one hundred or more years after his death, and the first edition of his work is vouched for as authentic and not posthumous, then one really has to suspend disbelief. In VI.74 Nostradamus predicts the death of Elizabeth I of England in 1603.

> La dechassee au regne tournera
> Ses ennemis trouvés des conjurés;
> Plus que jamais son temps triomphera
> Trois et septante à mort trop asseurés.

VI.74

She who was cast out will return to reign, her enemies found among conspirators. More than ever will her age be triumphant; at three and seventy to death very certainly.

Elizabeth was certainly rejected in her childhood, the subject and victim of a series of conspiracies during the reign of her sister, Mary Tudor. She died aged 70 in 1603, after a long and glorious reign. Most interpretations want to insert a comma between "trois et septante," indicating the first number as the year she died, (16)03 and the second as her age. If the reader is not convinced by this there are far more specific predictions. I am simply trying to put them forward in some sort of chronological order.

In 1607 Pope Urban VIII banned a notorious alchemistic treatise known as *Dekker's Almanach*, a book which greatly influenced English astrologers such as John Dee, Walter Raleigh and those who followed in the Hermetic tradition.

> *Croistra le nombre si grand des astronomes,*
> *Chassez, bannis et livres censurez,*
> *L'an mil six cents et sept par sacre glomes*
> *Que nul aux sacres ne seront asseurez.*
>
> VIII.71

> *The number of astrologers will grow so great that they will be driven out, banned and their books censored, in the year 1607, by sacred assemblies so that none will be safe from the holy ones.*

Perhaps this prediction is not earthshaking in its application, but one must remember how important astrology was to Nostradamus and those educated in his tradition. It certainly is accurate. The Pope banned *Dekker's Almanach* in 1607 under pain of expulsion from the Church, which caused a great deal of controversy.

Another prediction relating to the Vatican was dated 1609, and although not completely accurate, is close enough to warrant attention. In X.91 we learn:

> *Clergé Romain l'an mil six cens et neuf,*
> *Au Chef de l'an feras election.*
> *D'un gris et noir de la Compagne issu,*
> *Qui onc ne feut si maling.*

In the year 1609, the Roman clergy at the head of the year, will have an election for a leader. One gray and black, coming forth from Campania, there was never one as wicked as he.

Pope Paul V reigned in the Vatican from 1605 to 1621, so initially this prediction appeared erroneous. But he fell seriously ill in 1609, and according to contemporary letters and reports there was a great deal of intriguing between the Courts of France and Rome, should he die an inopportune death. The gray monks would be Franciscans and the black, Benedictines, both highly political orders at the time.

A more spectacular prediction was that of the Great Fire of London of 1666. It is to be remembered that during the sixteenth and seventeenth centuries it was common to write dates without the thousand prefix, i.e., 666 instead of 1666. This can still be seen on tombstones of the period. This device is used in II.51.

> *Le sang de juste à Londres sera faulte*
> *Brulés par fouldres de vingt trois les six;*
> *La dame antique cherra de place haute*
> *Des mesme secte plusieurs seront occis.*

II.51

The blood of the just will be demanded of London, burned by fire in three times twenty plus six. The ancient lady will fall from her high position and many of the same denomination will be killed.

One of the certain factors is that the only fire occurring in London in a year '66 is the Great Fire of 1666. The "dame antique" who falls is usually interpreted as the Cathedral of St Paul's which was destroyed as were many other churches of the Catholic faith. People fled from their wooden houses seeking shelter from the flames in the stone-built churches, but due to the intense heat even these buildings did not escape. The "blood of the just" probably refers to the fact that the victims of the fire were undeserving of their fate. This phrase is also used in II.53 when Nostradamus talks of a great plague in a maritime city "which will not stop until death is avenged by the blood of the just . . . the great lady is outraged by the pretense." This last line is almost certainly St. Paul's, the "dame antique" of II.51, outraged because Protestantism was soon afterward reintroduced to England under William III.

This next prediction not only gives the proper names of the parties concerned and the year, but also the actual month! The odds against this being chance must be astronomical.

> *Le tiers climat sous Aries comprins*
> *L'an mil sept cens vingt et sept en Octobre*
> *Le Roy de Perse par ceux d'Egypte prins:*
> *Conflit, mort, perte: à la croix grand oppobre.*
>
> *III.77*

At the third climate included under Aries in the year 1727, in October, the King of Persia captured by those of Egypt: battle, death, loss: great blame to the cross.

When I first read this quatrain I thought it was erroneous, but it is quite correct. In October 1727, an obscure peace treaty was concluded between the Turks and the Persians. Because Egypt belonged to the Ottoman Empire, Nostradamus uses it as a euphemism for the Turks.

The loss to the Cross, Christianity, is explained by the fact that the then Shah Asharaf gave the lands of Emvan, Tauris and Hamadan to the Turks in return for the recognition of his dynasty, and recognized the Sultan as the legitimate heir to the Caliph. No more Crusades were ever raised by the Christian Church and the Ottoman Empire went from strength to strength until this present century.

In the Epistle dedicated to Henri II which appears at the beginning of the second part of the Centuries, published in 1558, Nostradamus saw a persecution of the Church in France.

> *Et commençant icelle annee sera faite plus grande persecution à l'Eglise chretienne . . . et durera cette ici jusqu'à l'an mil sept cent nonante deux que l'on cuidera etre une renovation de siecle.*

> *Beginning with this year the Christian Church will be persecuted more fiercely and this will last up to the year 1792, which will be believed to mark a renewal of time.*

Nostradamus seems to see the progress of the French Revolution coming to a climax in 1792, as indeed it did. This was the year in which the mon-

archy was finally abolished, the Republic was proclaimed and the famous new calendar attempted.
This last may be taken as a renewal of time, (siecles).

Napoleon himself is mentioned not only by date
but also by name, as is his very particular personal
crest—the bees. Nostradamus calls him and his followers "the swarm of bees" in IV.26, in the only
quatrain that is written entirely in Provençal.

> *Lou grand eyssame se levera d'abelhos,*
> *Que non sauran don te siegen venguddos.*
> *De nuech l'embousque, lou gach dessous las*
>   *treilhos*
> *Cuitad trahido per cinq lengos non nudos.*

> *The great swarm of bees will arise, but no one will*
> *know where they have sprung from. The ambush by night,*
> *the sentinel under the vines, a city landed over by five*
> *tongues, not naked.*

This extraordinary quatrain describes in great
detail Napoleon's coup d'état of the 18th Brumaire
(9th November), 1799. Bees were Napoleon's emblem. They still can be seen on the tapestries and
chairs at Fontainebleau and Malmaison. The five
tongues (i.e., men who babble) who handed over
Paris were the five members of the Directory who
were bribed (non nudos) to give way to Napoleon's
Consulate. They were wearing their official clothes
as members of the Directory, which gives the expression a second meaning, a typical Nostradamus

device. The coup was planned the day before it took place. It is generally accepted that "las treilhos" is an anagram for the Tuileries into which Napoleon moved as soon as he saw his action had succeeded. The exact French equivalent is "treilles," trellis or lattice, but it is phonetically close enough to be acceptable.

In VIII.1, Napoleon is grandly mentioned in an anagram:

> *PAU NAY LORON plus feu qu'à sang sera*
> *Laude nager, fuire grand au surrez.*
> *Les agassas* entree refusera*
> *Pampon, Durance, les tiendra enserrez.*

> *PAU NAY LORON will be more of fire than blood, to swim in praise the great one to flee to the confluence [of the rivers]. He will refuse entrance to the magpies. Pampon and Durance will keep them confined.*

Although the first three words are all names of towns in western France, Nostradamus does seem to be talking of a man rather than places. The capital letters probably indicate a more fanciful reading by anagram. PAU NAY LORON becomes NAPAULON ROY, Napoleon the King. It was commonplace to spell Napoleon's name with an "au" rather than an "o" and anyway, sixteenth century orthography was very unreliable. The connection between the assegas, the magpies and Pius

---

*Agassas. Provençal: agassa, magpie, known in French as pie, which is also the French spelling of Pius, a pope. A typical Nostradamus pun.

would refer to the two Popes, Pius VI and VII, who were both imprisoned by Napoleon. The confluence of rivers refers to Valence where the Rhône and Isere meet and where Pius VI was taken to die in 1798–1799.

Pius VII was taken to Savona and then to Fontainebleau in 1782. Therefore one must admit that neither was imprisoned near the Durance of line 4. But Durance was close to Avignon, which belonged to the Vatican until 1791, and the rivers Rhône and Durance do meet there, so it is a reasonable interpretation through association.

An example of a prediction with the month and the date, coupled with a destructive event, in this case an assassination, can be found in III.96.

> *Chef de Fossan aura gorge coupee,*
> *Par le ducteur du limier et levrier;*
> *Le faict patré par ceux de mont Tarpee,*
> *Saturne en Leo 13 de fevrier.*

> **The leader from Fossano will have his throat cut by the man who exercises the bloodhounds and the greyhounds. The deed will be done by those of the Tarpean rock, when Saturn is in Leo on 13th February.**

It is difficult to trace the leader from Fossano. He could be the Duc of Berry whose maternal grandfather was the King of Fossano in Sardinia. The rest of the quatrain then fits very nicely into place. The assassin was Louvel, who worked in the royal stables. He was a Republican. In Ancient Rome, a republic, criminals were thrown off the Tarpean rock to their deaths. Saturn rules Aquarius and in astrological terms when it is in the opposite sign of Leo it must be understood as maleficent. The Duc de Berry was stabbed on 13 February 1820 when leaving the Opera, just as Nostradamus states.

A typical erroneous and failed quatrain is VI.54, in which Nostradamus gives a date and several proper names.

> *Au poinct du jour au second chant du coq,*
> *Ceulx de Tunes, de Fez, et de Bugie,*
> *Par les Arabes captif le Roi Maroq,*
> *L'an mil six cens et sept, de Liturgie.*

> *At daybreak at the second cockcrow, those of Tunis, Fez, and of Bougie; the Arabs captured by the King of Morocco in the year 1607 by the Liturgy.*

Technically, this should be a comparatively easy quatrain to break. It appears to predict the fall of the Ottoman Empire in 1607. No commentator seems to agree on what Nostradamus may mean by the extraordinary phrase, "by the Liturgy." It could be a simple equivalent of Anno Domini, but, as I have said, Nostradamus was usually more convoluted in his meanings.

An interesting characteristic which Nostradamus has in common with our contemporary prophets such as Edgar Cayce and Jeane Dixon, was that he was recognized during his lifetime as a talented predictor of close contemporary events. Jeane Dixon predicted both the J. F. Kennedy assassination and that of Martin Luther King, Jr. Nostradamus predicted in 1558 the even more unlikely death of his own king, Henri II (1.35), which happened in 1559.

Two very famous quatrains discuss the flight of Louis XVI and Marie Antoinette from Paris in 1791. Not only does Nostradamus comprehend the Revolution, but he gives the reader, without anagrams, the name of the obscure town in which the royal couple were caught and the even more obscure surname of the man in whose house they were staying at the time. These quatrains really are remarkable.

> *De nuict viendra par la forest de Reines*
> *Deux pars vaultort Herne la pierre blanche,*
> *Le moine noir en gris dedans Varennes*
> *Esleu cap, cause tempeste feu sang tranche.*
>
> *IX.20*

> By night will come through the forest of Reins two partners, by a roundabout route; the queen, the white stone. The monk-king dressed in gray at Varennes, the elected Capet causes tempest, fire and bloody slicing.

Louis XVI and his wife, Marie Antoinette, escaped from the Tuileries in Paris through a secret door to the queen's apartment. Their route took them through the forest of Reins, but they lost their way and took a roundabout road (vaultort). It is probable that pierre blanche refers to the notorious "affair of the diamond necklace" which demolished the queen's already fragile reputation among the French people. It may also refer to the phenomenon that the queen's hair turned white almost overnight after her capture, as reported by her ladies-in-waiting and the fact that she always wore white dresses. The king was disguised in a plain gray suit when they entered Varennes—the word moine may refer to that or to his earlier impotence. He was a Capet, the first elected, "esleu," King of France, and as Nostradamus says in the last line, was both the cause and the victim of the Revolution. The verb trancher means to slice and is particularly apposite in the context of the guillotine.

Although Nostradamus claims to have mixed up the quatrains in order to avoid the scrutiny of the Inquisition, various themes do tend to remain in the same century. He did not always separate the quatrains very accurately. Thus only fourteen quatrains later, IX.35, we find another very explicit one concerning Louix XVI and his flight to Varennes.

> *Le part solus mari sera mitré,*
> *Retour conflict passera sur le thuille*
> *Par cinq cens un trahir sera tiltré*
> *Narbonne et Saulce par couteaux avons d'huile.*
> IX.34

> *The partner, solitary but married, will be mitred; the return, worn by fighting he will pass through the Tuileries. By five hundred one traitor will be ennobled. Narbonne and Saulce, we will have oil for knives.*

This is, in effect, one of the most outstanding quatrains. When the royal couple, Louis XVI and Marie Antoinette, were stopped at Varennes (IX.20), they spent the night in the house of a man named Saulce. The Sauce family (modern spelling) have been chandlers and spice merchants there since the sixteenth century. The reference to the king being mitred and the Tuileries is a fascinating detail. Louis was returned to the Tuileries on June 20, 1792, when the mob invaded the palace and forced him to wear the revolutionary cap of liberty, which does look extraordinarily like a mitre. I think, as do some other commentators, that couteaux is a misprint for quartants—oil sold in retail—which is exactly what our eighteenth-century M. Saulce did. Thiers, in his *History of France,* states that when the mob returned to the Tuileries they numbered five hundred. Certainly this quatrain is full of typical Nostradamus detail.

Napoleon is often referred to as the Destroyer, the Thunderbolt, by Nostradamus. The Greek derivation of his name, NEAPOLLUN, means destroyer or exterminator, and in fact it was spelt in this way during his lifetime as can be seen on an inscription in the Place Vendôme of 1805 which reads, NEAPOLIO IMP. AUG.

In I.76 he is called "d'un nom farouche," of a barbaric name, and in IV.54:

> *D'un nom qui onques ne fut au Roy Gallois*
> *Jamais ne fut une fouldre si craintif:*

Tremblant l'Italie, l'Espagne et les Anglois
De femmes estrangiers grandement attentif.

Of a name which was never borne by a French king, there was never so fearful a thunderbolt. Italy, Spain and the English tremble. He will be greatly attentive to foreign women.

Napoleon certainly brought a new name, Bonaparte, to the line of French kings that he usurped. Most kings had shared the same names since Nostradamus' time: Louis (6), Henri (2), Charles (2), and Francis (2). The trembling of Europe and the English is self-explanatory. He was also very uxurious and enamored of both his foreign wives, the Créole Josephine and the Austrian Marie Louise. This may also contain a reference to his Polish mistress, Marie Walewska.

Napoleon's life is very succinctly put in two quatrains, I.32 and I.60.

Le grand Empire sera tost translaté
En lieu petit, qui bien tost viendra croistre:
Leu bien infime d'exigue comté,
Ou au milieu viendra poser son sceptre.

I.32

The great Empire will soon be exchanged for a small place, which soon begins to grow. An even smaller place of tiny area, in the middle of which he shall come to lay down his scepter.

The first thing to note in this quatrain is the use

of the "trigger word" Empire, not Kingdom, which is soon exchanged for the tiny island of Elba. But when Napoleon escapes and lives the victorious 100 days his Empire starts to grow again. But on his second defeat he is relegated to the even smaller island of St. Helena, where he puts down his scepter and relinquishes all claims to power. The "Emperor" theme is continued in I.60.

> *Un Empereur naistra pres d'Italie*
> *Qui à l'Empire sera vendu bien cher . . .*

> *An Emperor will be born near Italy who will cost the Empire very dearly . . .*

Napoleon was born in Corsica near Italy and the newfound Empire of France certainly paid for his military ambitions very dearly, both in manpower and political strength.

Nostradamus was a fervid royalist. His dislike of anything other than absolute monarchy comes over very clearly in the *Prophecies*. So when he writes of the unthinkable, a Parliament in London which will execute the king, he is describing something utterly shocking. It is not difficult to connect this with the execution of Charles I in 1649. Interestingly enough, the quatrain is also numbered 49— IX.49—but I think this is probably coincidence. ". . . Senat du Londres mettront à mort leur Roi . . ." He also seems to foresee the king's imprisonment in the Tower.

La forteresse aupres de la Tamise
Cherra par lors, le Roi dedans serré
Aupres du pont sera veu en chemise
Un devant mort, puis dans le fort barré.

VIII.37

The fortress near the Thames will fall when after an attack, the king is locked up inside. He will be seen in his shirt near the bridge, one before death, then barred within the fortress.

This quatrain is relevantly exact in its details. After his defeat and captivity Charles I was taken to Windsor Castle, overlooking the Thames, in December 1648, where he remained until January 1649. The castle "fell" because it came into the hands of the Parliamentarians. After his trial on January 30, Charles was wearing a white shirt when he went to his execution.

The founder of modern medicine, as he is often known, Louis Pasteur, was described both directly by name and indirectly by date by Nostradamus.

Perdu trouvé, caché de si long siecle,
Sera Pasteur demi Dieu Honoré:
Ains que la lune acheve son grand siecle,
Par autres vents sera deshonoré.

I.25

The lost thing, hidden for many centuries, is discovered. Pasteur will be celebrated as an almost godlike figure. This is when the moon completes her great cycle, but by other rumors he shall be dishonored.

Louis Pasteur founded the Institut Pasteur on November 14, 1889. The astrological cycle of the moon ran from 1539 to 1889, an accurate enough dating. Pasteur's discovery that germs polluted the atmosphere was one of the most important in contemporary theory, and helped lead to Lister's theory of sterilization. Even the *Encyclopaedia Britannica* acknowledges that Pasteur was a "demi Dieu," "the accepted head of the medical movement of the time." The "rumors of dishonor" consist of the opposition roused among older members of the Academy against such new practices as vaccination against hydrophobia.

I was not certain whether to insert the quatrains about Hitler, which are remarkably conclusive, into this chapter, or whether they deserve a chapter to themselves. However, since I have decided to encompass a few of Nostradamus' better "bull's eyes" in this chapter, before leading up to the postwar period and the present, they cannot be ignored.

Nostradamus regarded Hitler as the second antichrist, Napoleon being the first, and the third is to descend upon us all in the late 1980s. Those Hitler quatrains which write of him by name use the orthography Hifter—the long *l* or *f* being very ambiguous in the sixteenth century. Visually Hitler may with reason be written into this word—the letters are so alike.

The other descriptions of this man seem even more accurate. The reader must decide. I personally accept them, as much for the surrounding evidence, when I find he is termed "The Captain of Greater Germany," the Third Reich, and the "man of the croix gammé," the swastika, "the offspring of Germany who observes no law."

> *Bestes farouches de faim fleuves tranner*
> *Plus part du champ encore Hister sera*
> *En caige de fer le grand sera traisner*
> *Quand rien enfant de Germain observera.*

II.24

> *Beasts wild with hunger will cross the rivers, the greater part of the battle will be against Hitler. He will cause great men to be dragged in a cage of iron, when the son of Germany obeys no law.*

Even if one ignores the word Hister/Hitler, the last line seems to describe the Führer very clearly. Born in Austria, he was certainly an offspring of Germany proper. It is interesting that before the early 1930s most commentators believed Hister to mean the river Danube from its old Latin name of Ister. But many of these named quatrains certainly do not refer to a river, rather to a man who is a world force. Several quatrains link Hitler with England, which is geographically impossible if it is understood as the river.

What is so very important, and an example of the dangerous self-fulfilling aspect of prophecy, is that Hitler recognized himself in these quatrains very early on and Goebbels, his later Minister of Propaganda, was using them definitely by 1936. However, Goebbels was a fanatic believer in astrology through the influence of his wife, and it may be that he introduced his Führer to them indirectly. In 1939 an obscure book, *Mysterien von Sonne und Seele*, by Professor Hans-Herman Kritzinger, included a chapter on Nostradamus, which indicated that in 1939 a major crisis in Great Britain would coincide with a Polish one. Frau Dr. Goebbels drew her husband's attention to it and this fanned the flame of fervor in the Nazi believers. This incident, what led up to it and the tragic results to Ernst Krafft, Hitler's main astrologer, are vividly described by Ellic Howe in his book, *Nostradamus and the Nazis*. It is worthy of a chapter in itself, but since I am trying in this chapter simply to produce some evidence as to Nostradamus' validity in past prophecies, and then concentrate on the future, I must, very regretfully, neglect this fascinating sideline.

Events of Hitler's life seem very strongly documented.

> *Un capitaine de la grande Germanie,*
> *Se viendra rendre par simulé secours . . .*
>
> IX.90

> *A Captain of Greater Germany will come to deliver false help . . .*

This sounds uncannily like the Grossdeutsch land of Hitler's Third Reich. The line describing Hitler giving "false help" is very apt as it was under this excuse that he invaded Poland.

Quatrain III.58 seems to link up with this: it describes a man from Austria who becomes a great man of the people, "defending" Hungary and Poland, whose fate shall never be determined. Shades of the Bunker of Berlin?

> *Aupres du Rhin des Montaignes Noriques*
> *Naistra un grand de gens trop tard venu,*
> *Qui defendra Saurome et Panoniques*
> *Qu'on ne scaura qu'il sera devenu.*

III.58

> **Near the Rhine from the mountains of Norice, will be born a great man of the people, come too late. He will defend Poland, and Hungary, no one will ever know what happened to him.**

How many other dictators have gone to an undocumented death? There have always been doubts as to whether Hitler and his mistress, Eva Braun, committed suicide. There are numerous legends as to his fleeing through the notorious "Vatican route" to South America. There seems to be no other historical personage of note who is also associated with a crooked iron cross—the swastika: VI.49—"le croix par fer ne raffe ne riffe." A double irony here as the iron cross was a famous German decoration for valor. Nostradamus again! There are numerous "Hitler" quatrains but I would like to round off with one that seems to refer to his infamous alliance with Mussolini.

La liberté ne sera recouvree
L'occupera noir fier vilain inique:
Quand la matiere du pont sera ouvree
D'Hister, Venise fasché la republique.

V.29

Liberty will not be regained; it will be occupied by a black, proud, villainous and unjust man. When the matter of the Pope is opened by Hitler, the republic of Venice will be vexed.

Mussolini's intrigues to secure an alliance with Hitler during 1934–1938 are well documented. They eventually met in Venice, which by then was a republic and Mussolini its dictator. Nostradamus' details are interesting. Apart from the general meaning of black as bad are contained hints of the S.S. uniform and that of the black shirts, the Fascisti. The situation with the Pope (Pontifex) almost certainly refers to the Concordat drawn up between Mussolini and the Pope in 1928. It may also contain the implication that Pope Pius XII's attitude toward the Nazis was extremely ambiguous. He certainly opened an escape route for them to South America as I have already mentioned.

One of the best examples of the misuse or abuse of prophecy is that made by Hitler's astrologer, Ernst Krafft. Krafft had been forcibly detained, together with other students of the occult, to interpret Nostradamus, and the "Hister" quatrains in particular, in favor of the Führer. Eventually the scholar in him rebelled, and he died in a concentration camp in 1941. But before that he interpreted VI.51 as an attempt on Hitler's life in November 1939 and actually sent a telegram to the meeting Hitler was attending to alert him. In fact a bomb had been hidden in a pillar behind the rostrum and it was sheer chance that Hitler and his party left earlier than scheduled, thus avoiding being killed although other members of the assembly were severely wounded. This is the quatrain that Krafft believed prophesied an attempt to assassinate Hitler and which convinced the Führer himself beyond all doubt.

> *Peuple assemblé, voir nouveau expectacle,*
> *Princes et Rois par plusieures assistans*
> *Pilliers faillir, murs, mais comme miracle*
> *Le Roi sauvé et trente des instants.*

VI.51

The people are gathered to see a new spectacle. Princes and kings among many onlookers. The pillars, the walls fall, but as if by a miracle, the King and thirty of those present are saved.

I leave the interpretation of this to the reader but it is ironic that it made Krafft's reputation and confirmed Hitler's faith in Nostradamus' predictions. Double interpretation or misinterpretation of prophecy is one of the scholar's great problems. There is no doubt that some people are more sensitive to hidden meanings than others, but equally, perhaps those predictions may simply act as a trigger for the interpreter's latent talent for precognition. It is worth a thought. Another example of this form of double prediction is found in the extraordinary interpretations of Nostradamus by Abbé Torné. It is hard to believe but it is stated as fact that his periodic publications on Nostradamus influenced political opinion and caused France to erect the infamous Maginot line, which fell so quickly to the Germans in 1940. The particular quatrain runs as follows:

> *Pres du grand fleuve, grand fosse terre egeste,*
> *En quinze pars sera l'eau divisee*
> *La cité prinse, feu, sang, cris conflict mettre*
> *Et la plus part concerne au collisée.**

IV.80

> *Near the great river, a great trench, earth evacuated: the water will be divided into fifteen parts. The city is taken, fire, blood, cries and battles given, the greater part is to do with the collision [battle].*

James Laver certainly accepted the World War II interpretation. Hitler partially ignored the Maginot line and advanced on other fronts leading to the battles fought in France.

Nostradamus saw the downfall of the Spanish monarchy before the Second World War in I.31 engineered by a man he calls Franco: his astoundingly long and comparatively peaceful reign after

---

*Collisée. Latin: collisus—clash.

the decimation of the Civil War 1936–1939 when Spain determined to remain neutral during the Second World War. However, many commentators would regard this "neutral state" with a certain amount of skepticism.

> *De castel Franco sortira l'assemblee*
> *L'Ambassadeur non plaisant fera scisme*
> *Ceux de Ribiere seront en la meslee*
> *Et au grand goulphre desnier ont l'entree.*

IX.16

From Castile Franco will bring out the assembly, the ambassadors will not agree and cause a rift. Riviera's people will be in the crowd, and the great man will be denied entry to the Gulf.

Primo de Rivera (*b* and *v* are often confused phonetically) was the Spanish dictator whom Franco tried and eventually succeeded in deposing. For this the attempt Franco was exiled to Morocco and not allowed to cross the Mediterranean back into Spain until his return at the time of the Civil War. Franco and Mussolini "the dictator" are referred to as well in III.68.

It seems that prophets can sometimes force others to predict. How often their warnings have been understood is impossible to know. Nevertheless it does seem that their foreknowledge cannot be totally denied, even if in general we only recognize those alarms that are missed by contemporaries.

6 ENIGMATIC QUATRAINS: 1945–1980

This was one of the hardest chapters to write. When one has a definite text like St. Augustine or Thomas More one is left in little doubt as to their meaning, subject to nothing more than very subtle variations. But here I came across a large number of Nostradamus' quatrains, all of which seem realistic enough to deserve inclusion, but which have no linking theme whatsoever. It really is the writer's as well as the editor's nightmare. I feel that each quatrain is important in its own right, but very often bears no connection with any other subject. The sequence of three definite and two very dubious quatrains about the fate of the British monarchy is about the strongest. So all I can do is beg the readers' indulgence. If this chapter irritates, all I can recommend is that you continue on to the more conventional ones that follow. Equally, I feel that if I had omitted it, which I was tempted to do, many Nostradamus experts would feel I was cheating. All I can say is that Nostradamus published all the quatrains I have used and presumably wished them to be known. It has been very hard to be selective about them, and any reader wishing to know more should read the whole of the text of the *Prophecies.*

Many quatrains repeat the same theme, but I have tried not to allow myself the luxury of repetition, space and reader's boredom. However, many of these odd quatrains were solved, or partially so, by the many letters from my readers, for which I am grateful.

NOSTRADAMUS' BELIEF IN VALIDITY AND MEANINGS OF PHENOMENA

This is one of my favorite quatrains when all one's fantasies about prediction and phenomena are allowable!

> *Laict, sang, grenouilles escoudre en Dalmatie,*
> *Conflict donné, peste pres de Balennes*
> *Cri sera grand par toute Esclavonie,*
> *Lors naistra monstre pres et dedans Ravenne.*
>
> *II.32*

> *Milk, blood, frogs will be prepared in Dalmatia.*
> *Battle engaged, plague near Balennes. A great city will*

go up throughout Slavonia—then a monster will be born near Ravenna.

AUTHENTICATED SHOWERS OF
MILK, BLOOD AND FROGS

This prophecy covers both sides of the Adriatic. Showers of milk, blood and frogs have all been authenticated in recent times. In 1954 at Sutton Park, Birmingham, England, people sheltering from the rain were bombarded by hundreds of little frogs bouncing off umbrellas and scaring everyone with their leaping around. It is an interesting fact that whenever one of these "frog falls" appears the fall is never of full-grown frogs or of tadpoles. Another such case happened in Arkansas on January 2, 1983, when a group of men playing golf were deluged with "thousands of frogs about the size of nickels which came right down with the rain from the sky." Rains of blood are among one of the oldest prodigies known to man, yet people still regard them as a myth. In Brazil on August 27, 1968, a shower of blood and scraps of meat fell for between five to seven minutes over an area of one square kilometer between Cocpava and São José dos Campos. These were analyzed as being human flesh, yet no airplane crash occurred anywhere in the vicinity at the time. It was an extraordinary incident, without visible explanation. There have also been instances of colored rain. Professor Brun of

Geneva investigated a case of blood-rain in 1880 in Morocco and found the rocks and vegetation at Djebel-Sekra covered with dried red scales which were identified as remains of colonies of a minute organism called Protococcus Fluvialis. His explanation was that they had been deposited by a whirlwind but he could not explain away the extraordinary selection involved. The whole colony was composed entirely of young organisms. Dalmatia is on the Eastern Adriatic, Balennes was Trebula, Balliensis near Capua, Ravenna is in Central Italy. The former province of Slavonia is now part of northern Yugoslavia and part of the Hungarian Empire.

NOSTRADAMUS THE DOCTOR

Ce que vivra et n'ayant ancien sens,
Viendra leser à mort son artifice:
Austun, Chalan, Langres et les deux Sens,
La gresle et glace fera grand malefice.

I.22

A thing that exists without any original senses will cause its own end to happen through artifice. At Autun, Chalan, Langres and Sens . . .

RARE MEDICAL EVENT, 1613

A very interesting solution to the quatrain occurred

in Garancières, the first English commentator on Nostradamus. He states that in 1613 a petrified embryo was removed by operation (artifice) from the womb of a woman called Columba Chantry who lived at Sens. This was quite a rare event: examples can be found in medical textbooks, and a woman living in Italy two years ago was found to have been carrying a petrified embryo well into her sixties; an interesting medical sidelight on Nostradamus the doctor. All the towns mentioned belong to the Duchy of Burgundy. The reference to the weather seems very general, the quatrain implying that it occurred around the same period, 1613. The second town of Sens is near Louhans.

PRODUCTION OF ARTIFICIAL RAIN

De nuict par Nantes L'Iris apparoistra,
Des artz marins susciteront la pluie:
Arabique goulfre grand classe parfondra,
Un monstre en Saxe naistra d'ours et truie.

VI.44

By night the rainbow will appear near Nantes, the marine arts will raise up rain. In the Arabian Gulf a great fleet will founder. In Saxony a monster will be born of a bear and a sow.

This quatrain may apply to the twentieth century. In 1947, scientists discovered how to produce artificial rain (line 2). At a time when a rainbow ap-

pears at Nantes a fleet will meet disaster either in
the Red Sea, since there is no actual Gulf of Arabia,
or in the Arabian Sea, which lies to the south, or the
Persian Gulf to the east. It seems to indicate a
strong naval presence in this area—could this be a
confrontation between the Ayatollah and Iraq or
the recent shelling of ships in the Gulf by Iran?

INTERESTING SCIENTIFIC REVELATION. GREEK FIRE

La legion dans la marine classe,
Calcine, Magnes souphre et poix bruslera:
Le long repos de l'asseuree place,
Port Selyn, Hercle feu les consumera.

IV.23

    The legion in the marine fleet will burn, lime,
magnesia, sulphur and pitch. The long rest in a safe
place; Port Selin, Monaco will be consumed by fire.

This is a very strange quatrain. The second line
appears to be giving a recipe for Greek fire, the
famous "secret weapon" of the Greeks and Byzan-
tines. Nostradamus is quite correct because after
much research, Lieutenant Colonel H. Hime said
that it was the presence of quicklime which distinguished Greek fire from all other known incendi-
aries of the period. The mixture gave rise to heat
on contact with water and thus took fire spon-
taneously when wet and was used with great success

in sea battles. But again, Port Selin, if I am correct in identifying it with Genoa, and Monaco, have not been attacked since Nostradamus' day. But the port of Toulon was used by Barbarossa when he helped the French against the emperor during the 1540s, so Nostradamus would have been writing in retrospect, not predicting.

PHENOMENA

La magna vaqua à Ravenne grand trouble,
Conduictz par quinze enserrez à Fornase
A Rome naistre deux monstres à teste double
Sang, feu, deluges, les plus grands à l'espase.

IX.3

The magna vaqua near Ravenna in great trouble,
led by fifteen shut up at Fornese; at Rome two monsters
with double heads are born, blood, fire, floods, the greatest
in the air.

This seems to be involved with the Papal states and the Vatican, together with hanging and two-headed monsters, two of which were shown to Nostradamus in his capacity of prophet in the early 1560s near Salon, when he declared them to predict a disunited France to come. When one considers that France had survived one religious war in 1562–3 with another seven to follow, this does not seem to need great clairvoyance on Nostradamus' part. I wonder if the two-headed monster refers to the two de'Medici cousins, both of whom obtained the Papacy through corruption? Leo X, Gianni, and Giulio who became Clement VII were both influential in the future of France as being uncles of Catherine de'Medici who married Henri II of France.

MARXISM

There are several general quatrains on what might reasonably be described as Marxist or Communist doctrine and surprisingly leading to its eventual decline, although this may only have been wishful thinking on Nostradamus' part. On the surface this one is not particularly obvious. Nostradamus is being a little more subtle than usual.

> *France a cinq pars par neglect assaille*
> *Tunis, Argel esmuez par Persiens:*
> *Leon, Seville, Barcelonne faille*
> *N'aura la classe par les Venetiens.*

> *I.73*

Francia shall be accused of negligence by five partners. Tunis and Algiers shall be stirred up by the Persians. Seville and Barcelona having failed, they will not have the fleet because of the Venetians.

Nostradamus does not make it clear who the five partners are, but it is interesting to note the reference to troubles between Middle Eastern countries and the Persians. In his day Iran was part of the

Ottoman Empire, an area of which is now part of the U.S.S.R. By implication Nostradamus feels that the Russians are mixed up in the Middle Eastern troubles. Four hundred years later it is beyond dispute.

Perhaps Marxism is again referred to here?

> *Avant long temps le tout sera rangé,*
> *Nous esperons un siecle bien senestre*
> *L'estat des masques et des seuls bien changé,*
> *Peu trouverant qu'a son rang vueille estre.*
>
> *II.10*

> *Before long everything will be organized: we await a very evil century. The state of the masked [Marxist?] and the solitary ones being greatly changed, few will find that they wish to retain their rank.*

I almost deleted this on writing because in most ways it fits the description of the fate of the eighteenth-century French nobility better than that of the U.S.S.R. But the closeness, so typical of Nostradamus, between "masques" and Marxist inclines me to leave it to the reader's judgment.

Here is another on the subject, somewhat more astonishing. The prophet seems to feel that the basic tenets of Marxism will fail, as indeed they already have in many ways. One would have to be a fool to think that its meritocracy has led to any form of equality.

> *Es lieux et temps chair au poisson donra lieu,*
> *La loi commune sera faicte au contraire:*

Vieux tiendra fort plus osté du millieu,
Le Pánta chiona philòn mis fort arriere.

IV.32

In those times and places that meat gives way to
fish the common law will be dictated in opposition. The old
[men?] will hold strong. Then removed from the scene: all
things common between friends put behind them.

Pánta chiona philòn is the Greek term for things
held in common between friends or equals, Communism in its purest sense perhaps? Its appeal obviously fades and the comment about the "old"
holding and ruling is ironic when one looks at the
age of an average member of the Politbureau and
the election of the new Soviet premier Konstantin
Chernenko, who is in his seventies.

NOSTRADAMUS: COMPREHENSION OF THE FUTURE POWER OF WRITTEN PROPAGANDA

Un qui des dieux d'Annibal infernaux,
Fera renaistre, effrayeur des humains:
Oncq' plus d'horreur ne plus dire journaulx,
Qu'avint viendra Babel aux Romains.

II.30

A man revives the infernal Gods of Hannibal, the
terror of mankind. Never more horror, nor do the papers
ever talk of worse things . . .

What is so interesting here is the fact that there were no newspapers as we understand them in Nostradamus' time, only pamphlets and books which were for the rich, both rare and expensive. The prophet seems to understand the power of the written word and the horror it can convey. Indeed he himself made use of it by writing the *Prophecies*.

OIL

Las qu'on verra grand peuple tourmenté
Par la loi saincte en totale ruine,
Par autres loix toute la Chestienté
Quand d'or, d'argent, trouve nouvelle mine.

I.53

Alas how we see a great nation sorely troubled and the holy law put into utter ruin. All Christianity, governed by different laws, when for gold and silver they discover a new source of wealth.

Oil has been the great strength and weapon of the Middle Eastern countries, indeed it still is. Much of the arms sent there come from the U.S.S.R. under oil trade agreements. Britain has been lucky with her North Sea oil fields, but they are finite and unfortunately more costly to maintain. By definition, therefore, gold and silver are not the only sources of wealth as they were understood to be in Nostradamus' time.

TYPICAL EXAMPLE OF FUTURISTIC WEAPONS

Par feu du ciel la cité presque aduste,
L'urne menace encor Ceucalion . . .

II.81

The city is almost burned down by fire from the sky, water again threatens Ceucalion [amost certain misprint for Deucalion].

A gentle description compared with what is to follow. Death inside globes of dreaded fear. Whatever object Nostradamus visualizes here it is certainly no cannon ball but some object of modern warfare, probably atomic because of the dreaded "mort caché" over and above the usual fire and destruction. The fates of Nagasaki and Hiroshima seem to have been glimpsed by him:

Aupres des portes et dedans deux cités
Seront deux fléaux et oncques n'apperceu un tel:
Faim, dedans peste, de fer hors gens boutés,
Crier secours au grand Dieu immortel.

II.6

Near the harbor and in two cities will descend two scourges the like of which have never been seen before. Hunger, plague within, people thrown out by the iron thing [sword?] will cry out for help from the great immortal God.

Both the cities of Nagasaki and Hiroshima are on the sea and experienced the first world plague of death by atomic radiation, something which had never been used openly against mankind before then. Notice how Nostradamus describes the radiation as being the plague within, "dedans peste." The plague endemic in southern France during Nostradamus' day was defined as the "charbon" because its victims became covered with large black pustules. Radiation burns turn black too. The last line speaks for itself.

There is one other worrying quatrain on this subject that may not yet have been fulfilled, or hopefully I have misinterpreted it. It implies that a small atomic bomb will be let loose somewhere in Greece or the Balkans, and of course, would tie in very well with our present-day Middle Eastern troubles.

> *Dans les cyclades, en perinthe et larisse,*
> *Dedans Sparte tout le Pelloponnesse:*
> *Si grand famine, peste par faux connisse,*
> *Neuf mois tiendra et tout le chevronesse.*

> V.90

In the Cyclades, Perinthius and Larissa, in Sparta and all the Peloponnesus: a very great famine, plague through false [i.e. man-made] dust. It will last nine months throughout the whole peninsula.

The only question I can ask is, what is "false dust"? Nostradamus knew obvious things like gunpowder, plague and usual medical troubles. This implies something more to him. Could it refer to fallout?

OPTIMISTIC VIEW OF FUTURE AFTER WAR?

Mars et le sceptre se trouvera conjoinct,
Dessoubz Cancer calamiteuse guerre:
Un peu apres sera nouveau Roi oingt,
Qui par long temps pacifiera la terre.

VI.24

Mars and the scepter will be in conjunction: A calamitous war under Cancer: A short time afterward a new king will be anointed who will bring peace to the earth for a long time.

This is one of Nostradamus' vaguely hopeful predictions, but at least he does hint at a time of peace. However, technically we have had the longest "world peace" this century already since World War II. Perhaps we should not allow ourselves to be too cynical? The scepter here stands for Jupiter, so this may be another prediction concerning the war Nostradamus foresees during the 1980s which will be followed by an era of peace.

Soleil levant un grand feu l'on verra
Bruit et clarté vers Aquilon tendants:
Dedans le rond mort et cris l'on orra
Par glaive, feu, faim, mort las attendants.

II.91

At sunrise a great fire will be seen, noise and light extending toward the north. Within the globe [sphere] death and cries are heard, death awaiting them through weapons, fire and famine.

This verse seems to imply that a country in the
northern hemisphere will be bombed suddenly at
dawn. The northern theme fits in with other of
Nostradamus' predictions. It will be followed by a
period of great devastation. In I.92, Nostradamus
states that although America will finally be victorious it may suffer the greatest destruction. A
gloomy prospect.

There is little optimism in Nostradamus' writing
but perhaps this quatrain has something to offer
us, despite the last line.

> *Nouveau venus lieu basti sans defence.*
> *Occuper la place par lors inhabitable:*
> *Pres, maisons, champs, villes prendre à*
> *   plaisance,*
> *Faim, Peste guerre arpen long labourable.*
>
> *II.19*

> The newcomers will build a place without de-
> fenses, occupying a place uninhabitable until then.
> Meadows, houses, field, towns will be lived in with plea-
> sure. Famine, plague and war, extensive arable land.

TWO SPACE QUATRAINS

> *Si grand Famine par unde pestifere.*
> *Par pluie longue le long du polle arctique,*
> *Samarobrin cent lieux de l'hemisphere,*
> *Vivront sans loi exempt de pollitique.*
>
> *VI.5*

A very great famine [caused] by a pestilent wave
will extend its long rain the length of the Arctic pole.
Samarobrin, one hundred leagues from the hemisphere:
they will live without law, exempt from politics.

This quatrain makes me slightly worried. In Cyrillic
Russian the word Samorobin is derived from two
words—Samo, self, and Robin, operator. This does
imply an unmanned satellite. Modern Soviet aircraft are known as Samoylot, which means self-
flying in Russian. I am indebted to Dr. John A.
Morris of Brunel University, England, for this ingenious interpretation. The rain is probably some
type of atomic or nuclear contamination.

Dedans le coing de luna viendra rendre,
Ou sera prins et mis en terre estrange,
Les fruitz immeurs seront à la grand esclandre
Grand vitupere à l'un grande louange.

IX.65

He will take himself to the corner of Luna, then
captured and placed on foreign territory. The unripe fruit
will be subject of great scandal, great blame; to the other
great praise.

If luna is to be taken literally as the moon, this
quatrain makes surprising sense. The first astro-
naut to land on the moon will most certainly be
taken and placed on a foreign land, "taken" in his
space capsule. The unripe fruit probably indicates
the great trouble, as America had with Apollo 13—
the rockets were not functioning properly and the

efforts to return the astronauts to earth were certainly the cause of scandal, blame and praise. It was admitted that the odds of their returning safely were extremely low. It is believed that the U.S.S.R. has suffered even greater losses of men in space, but officially these experiments are not on record.

POST–THIRD WORLD WAR SHIFT OF WORLD POWER CENTERS

The first two lines of this quatrain sound very modern through the very scope of their world-wide concept.

> *Le neuf empire en desolation*
> *Sera changé du pole aquilonaire.*

VIII.81

> *The New Empire in desolation will be moved from the Northern Pole.*

I had an interesting conversation some years ago with a scientist who was then working at Jodrell Bank, England, and he said that if there were severe atomic warfare, the South Pole, places like the Falklands would be the safest, taking into account sea and wind currents. It seems interesting to think of the White House based on some bleak sheep-ridden hill and a British Colony to boot!

SERIES ON THE FATE OF THE BRITISH EMPIRE

Le grand empire sera par Angleterre,
Le pempotam des ans plus de trois cens:
Grandes copies passer par mer et terre,
Les Lusitains n'en seront pas contens.

X.100

There will be a great English Empire, all powerful for more than three hundred years. Great forces cross by land and sea. The Portuguese will not be pleased.

These are a fascinating series of quatrains because although Britain was a political force to be reckoned with at the time Nostradamus wrote, she had neither the power nor the resources of Spain, France or the Holy Roman Empire. It is as though he foresaw her might by the time of the nineteenth century. Nostradamus foresees the British Empire lasting approximately three hundred years. Most interpreters take it as starting in the reign of Elizabeth I and going through to that of Victoria, fifty years or so longer than actually predicted. Line three is presumably obvious but the ambiguity as to the Portuguese I cannot solve. Typical of the Prophet to end his predictions (this is the last one) on such a note.

However, he is a little more specific about the fate of the British Empire in the following:

Sept fois changer verrez gent Britannique
Taintz en sang en deux cents nonante an:

Franche non point par appuy Germanique,
Aries doubte son pole Bastarnien.

III.57

Seven times the British nation will be seen to
change, soaked in blood in two hundred and ninety years.
Not at all free through German connections Aries fears for
the protectorate of Poland.

The great problem for this verse is to find the date
from which to calculate the 290 years and the seven
great changes which affect Britain. If the year 1603
is taken as the starting point, quite arbitrarily, the
whole verse fits, including the last line which clearly
links Poland (Bastarnien) with Britain in some
manner connected with a war. Aries, the first sign
of the Zodiac, rules the East. Nostradamus indicates that there will be a critical state of affairs in
Poland at the same time as Britain faces a great
crisis connected with Germany. It also implies that
the royal family on the throne at that time will be
the last British dynasty of any note. This may mean
that Prince Charles, a Battenberg by origin, will be
the last king on the English throne. If an astrological dating is taken, the planet Pluto has a 265-
year cycle which will next end in 1995, the new era
of peace given by Nostradamus as a specific date in
X.72. Therefore, the seven-year cycle should be
presumed to start in 1730. Politically it does not
seem all that improbable despite those who will sen-
timentalize over the fate, or maybe fortune, of the
young Princes, William and Henry.

When I translated the next quatrain for each of the various editions I have worked upon over the last ten years I dismissed it, saying that it was impossible to conceive of any son of the royal line being directly involved in a battlefront, and in an airplane. Since Prince Andrew's actions in the Falklands and the fact that his job was a pilot I can only offer the following quatrain. Whether he will suffer a minor wound in some future engagement is debatable, but the whole concept is somewhat astounding.

> *Un prince Anglais Mars a son coeur de ciel,*
> *Voudra poursuivre sa fortune prospere:*
> *Des deux duelles l'un percera le fiel*
> *Häi de lui, bien aimé de sa mere.*

III.16

An English Prince, War has his heart in the sky, will wish to follow his prospering fortune. In two duels [battles] one, hated by him, will pierce him the gallbladder, but he is well loved by his mother.

PRINCESS ANNE AND MARK PHILIPS

I have to admit that I do not consider that either of the following quatrains refer to Princess Anne and her husband. However, just as in the quatrain about Princess Grace of Monaco, I have had such an overwhelming amount of letters on the subject that I feel I should probably include them. I per-

sonally feel that "Dannemarc" is not an anagram
but a simple naming of modern Denmark. This is
one of the areas where I feel that people's
attempted interpretation of prophecy sometimes
verges somewhat on the lunatic.

> *Viendront livrer le Prince Dannemarc,*
> *Rachat honni au temple d'Artemide.*

> *IV.27*

> They will come to deliver the Prince of Denmark, a
shameful ransom to the temple of Artemis.

The latter is, of course, one of the aspects of the
Goddess of Love. This is presumed to be a "shameful ransom" because Princess Anne married a com-
moner, Captain Mark Philips.

> *Le second chef du regne d'Annemarc,*
> *Par Ceux de Frise et l'isle Britannique*
> *Fera despendre plus de cent mille marc . . .*

> *VI.41*

> The second leader during the reign of Annemarc
[Anne being the second child of Elizabeth II?] through the
people of Frisia and those of the British Isles will spend
more than one hundred thousand marks . . .

I cannot but maintain that both these quatrains re-
fer to Philip of Spain, husband of Queen Mary of
England who, at the time of Nostradamus was ruler
both of England and Frisia. But he did not possess
Denmark. That is the problem. The British Royal
Family have close blood and social ties with them.

The second son could refer again to Prince Andrew. His life-style seems somewhat extravagant compared with most of the Royals, who are more discreet. I do not think this refers to a second son of Princess Anne and Captain Mark Philips.

INFLATION

Les simulacres d'or et d'argent enflez,
Qu'apres le rapt au lac furent gettez
Au desouvert estaincts tous et troublez.
Au marbre script prescript intergetez.

VIII.28

The copies of gold and silver inflated, which after the theft were thrown into the lake, at the discovery that all is exhausted and dissipated by the debt. All scripts and bonds will be wiped out.

This quatrain may well be describing the monetary inflation which hit Europe during the 1920s and again in the last decades. It is one of the few quatrains I have not translated literally as it is too complex, and have used that of Dr. Fontbrune (1939). It is an interesting idea for a man who lived long before paper money (the copies of gold and silver) was ever used. Another possible suggestion is that the money "thrown into the lake" was part of the vast plundered Nazi fortunes that have never been recovered.

THE FATE OF PRINCESS GRACE OF MONACO

I have to admit that I am not really convinced by the interpretation I here offer to this quatrain. But since the death of the princess I have received such a remarkable number of letters from readers who were convinced of its meaning, that I include it for the readers' interest, if nothing else. Certainly the first line has relevance to any century.

> *De sang et faim plus grand calamité,*
> *Sept fois s'appreste à la marine plage:*
> *Monech de faim, lieu pris, captivité,*
> *Le grand mené croc en ferree caige.*

> *III.10*

> *With blood and famine even greater calamity; seven times it approaches the seashore. Monaco, from hunger, captured, in captivity. The great golden one caught, in an iron cage.*

Princess Grace, of the golden movies, the golden hair and golden life died in the iron cage of her crashed car. However, whether she could really be described as "great" I feel to be in question. Monaco, after all, is a very minor principality, and she achieved nothing that could be honestly called of international worth except for the few films she made in Hollywood.

RUSSIAN NAVAL POWER

Apres combat et bataille navale,
Le grand Neptune à son plus haut befroi:
Rouge adversaire de peur viendra pasle
Mettant le grand Ocean en effroi.

III.1

After the combat and naval battle, great Neptune in his highest belfry: the red adversary will become pale with fear, putting the great ocean into a state of terror.

This quatrain may refer to the enormous sea power being built up by Russia at the present time. "Neptune in his highest belfry" should be interpreted as a great sea battle. Strangely enough Nostradamus sees Russia, the red adversary, becoming pale with fear, although it is Russia which commences the war and creates terror on the high seas. He does not indicate on which side the victory will lie. This becomes more worrying when one thinks of the present deployment of the U.S. fleet in the eastern Mediterranean, and the continuous "odd" news stories that turn up about Russian trawlers or submarines out of their normal territory and equipped with immensely sophisticated instrumentation and presumably weaponry.

This is another quatrain which made little sense when the book was first written but which now appears much clearer. It reiterates the connection that Nostradamus believed to exist between France and the Middle East, and the Libyan reference is almost certainly one to President Qaddafi and his influence in the West, due to his involvement with the Palestinians, his new alliance with Syria and the oil problems of the West. Still further we have the problems in Chad, late 1984, where the Libyans appear to have reneged on the treaty of November 1984 with President Mitterrand of France. The reference to a translation from Arabic to French is puzzling, as Algeria was French and has now become a country in its own right. The first French-Arabic dictionary appeared in 1505, but I cannot think of any other work of literary merit that was translated under these conditions.

> *Prince libinique puissant en Occident,*
> *François d'Arabe viendra tant enflammer,*
> *Scavans aux lettres sera condescendant,*
> *La langue Arabe en François translater.*

III.27

The Libyan prince will be powerful in the West, the French will become so enamored of Arabia; learned in letters he will condescend to translate the Arab language into French.

This may indicate a strong union of both language and custom. The French influence in Northern Africa was vast, and is still very important.

SWISS BANK NEUTRALITY BROKEN

Swiss banks have always, as everyone knows, had

the reputation of guarding the privacy of their clients' affairs above all else. However, recent criminal and other prosecutions have caused them to release private documents to courts and relevant officials. Perhaps this is what Nostradamus was referring to in this quatrain?

> *Leur grand amus de l'exile malefice,*
> *Fera Sueve ravir leur grand contract*

> *I.61*

> The great amount of ill will created by those in exile will make the Swiss break their important agreement.

Since the only other really "important agreement" of the Swiss is their declared neutrality in times of war, financial revelations seem the more likely explanation. It might be presumed that "those in exile" refers to the many people who have broken the law and used Swiss bank accounts to cope with their finances.

NOSTRADAMUS PERSONAL DATING OF PUBLICATION AND COMPLETION OF PROPHECIES

> *Vingt ans du regne de la lune passez,*
> *Sept mil ans autre tiendra sa monarchie:*
> *Quand le soleil prendra ses jours lassez,*
> *Lors accomplit et mine ma prophetie.*

> *I.48*

When twenty years of the moon's reign have passed, another shall take up his rule for seven thousand years. When the exhausted Sun takes up his cycle, then my prophecy and threats shall be accomplished.

According to Roussat, the cycle of the moon lasted from 1535–1889, which places the date of the first line as 1555, the publication date of the first part of the Centuries. Nostradamus seems to envisage another 7000 years from that date to the cycle of the sun when all will be accomplished. According to astrologers we have now entered the reign of Aquarius. This quatrain is interesting in that it gives the date of publication and associates this with the completion of the prophecies. It is as though Nostradamus believes the Centuries are written at the start of a new era lasting 7000 years. It was a commonly held theory in the Middle Ages that the world would come to an end at the beginning of the seventh millennium. This information originated from the book of Enoch, which was general reading during the early centuries but removed by the Church from the Canon in A.D. 300. Nostradamus also refers to 7000 years in quatrain X.74 but no commentator is able to agree on the date from which to start calculating, and this theory does not agree with the statements of some of the other prophecies.

THE SLAUGHTER OF THE ISRAELI ATHLETES IN 1980

An revolu du grand nombre septiesme
Apparoistra au temps Jeux d'Hecatombe,
Non esloigne du grand eage milliesme
Que les entres sortiront de leur tombe.

X.74

The year of the great seventh number accomplished it will appear at the time of the games of slaughter not far from the age of the great millennium, when the dead will come out of their graves.

This slightly ambiguous quatrain possibly refers to the slaughter of the Israeli athletes at the Olympic Games in 1976—when the great seventh number, i.e., decade, is accomplished. But it could mean after the end of the decade. An appalling incident which should not be allowed to be forgotten. The next games were held in Los Angeles in 1984. No dead came out of their graves but the almost total boycott of the 1984 games by the Soviet bloc certainly changed their entire concept. Perhaps "shades of the dead" might be more appropriate.

ENOSIS AND PRESIDENT MAKARIOS

This quatrain may possibly describe Cyprus during the 1950 troubles when union with Greece was the

overwhelming local political issue. (I am not implying it is a dead one now.)

> *En ce temps là sera frustrée Cypres,*
> *De son secours de ceux de mer Egee:*
> *Vieux trucidez, mais par mesles et lyphres*
> *Seduict leur Roy, Royne plus outragee.*
>
> *III.89*

> *At that time Cyprus will be deprived of its help*
> *from those of the Aegean Sea. Old men slaughtered, but by*
> *cannons and supplications, the king is won over, the*
> *queen more outraged.*

The verse does seem to show that Cyprus will not
attain complete union with Greece, that the king
(Constantine?) will have been misled, and the
queen, probably the more unpopular Frederika,
will be greatly upset by their enforced exile in England. "Old men slaughtered" may well refer to the
assassination attempts upon the late Archbishop
Makarios and his eventual death.

VIETNAM

There seems to be only one really specific reference
to the tragedy of Vietnam.

> *Les dieux feront aux humains apparence,*
> *Ce qu'il seront auteurs de grand conflict:*
> *Avant ciel veu serein espée et lance*
> *Que vers main gauche sera plus grand afflict.*
>
> *I.91*

The gods will make it appear to mankind that they are the originators of a great war. Before, the sky was seen to be free of weapons and rockets: the greatest damage will be inflicted on the left side.

The type of weaponry makes it almost definitively a twentieth-century quatrain—particularly the "lances," rockets in the sky. The country on the left-hand side of the map, i.e., the West, is here declared to be the loser, and this must presumably be America, whose only, but spectacular defeat in this century occurred in Vietnam. There are no "trigger words" to link this with Perse or the antichrist, the war with whom he declares will be won by "Amorique."

ZIMBABWE/RHODESIA

La foy Punicque en Orient rompue
Grand Jud et Rosne, Loire et Tag changeront.
Quand du mulet la faim sera repue,
Classe espargie, sang et corps nageront.

II.60

Faith with Africa is broken in the East, Great Jordan, Rhone, Loire and Tagus will change. When the hunger of the mule is sated the fleet is scattered and bodies swim in blood.

Could line one refer to the governmental talks between Britain and the Africans in September to December 1979? At the time of these troubles the great rivers of Jordan in the Middle East, the Rhone and Loire in France, the Tagus in Spain and

Portugal will suffer political changes. This may mean the borders of the parent countries change, and is in some way allied to a great naval disaster. These are extremely obscure except for the interesting linking up of Jordan with Palestine, with reference to the talks held between King Hussein of Jordan and President Carter of the United States and his meeting in Novemer 1984 with the P.L.O.

The fleet may contain a reference to the massive number of ships and aircraft carriers sent by President Reagan to the eastern Mediterranean. The fate of the PLO is now a very different kettle of fish with Arafat's brilliant propaganda move releasing thousands of hostages and forming an alliance with Egypt. That area of conflict may have shifted but it is certainly not dead.

THE GRADUAL FAILURE OF THE LEAGUE OF NATIONS

Du lac Leman les sermons fascheront,
Les Jours seront reduicts par les sepmaines:
Puis mois, puis an, puis tous deffailliront,
Les magistrats damneront leurs loix vaines.

I.47

The strictures from Lake Geneva will annoy—from days they will be dragged out into weeks, then months, then years, then all will fail. The magistrates will damn their useless laws.

The gradual ineffectiveness of the League of Nations, based on Lake Geneva, is described very clearly. After years of fruitless argument and failure it was formally disbanded after World War II in August 1947, although many would claim it ceased to be effective by 1940.

NATO AND ITS FAILURE

Le camp Ascap d'Europe partira,
S'adjoignant proche de l'isle submergée:
D'Arton classe phalange pliera,
Nombril du monde plus grand voix subrogée.

II.22

The aimless army will depart from Europe, and join up close to the submerged island. The NATO fleet folds up its standard, and navel of the world taken over by a greater voice.

Nostradamus writes of the submerged island again in IX.31, where it is identified with Britain. The army is described as aimless; could this mean that it, just like the NATO fleet, had no warlike intent as they were both only on exercises? This view is reinforced by the fact that the fleet folds up its standards showing no signs of war. The navel of the world, and its center, may be understood as Italy, presumably the center of the direction of operations. But again, Nostradamus implies that NATO will be taken over (subrogée) by a more powerful agency. European countries do combine at the present time to hold naval and military exercises both in Europe and in the English Channel under the auspices of NATO. Both America and Britain are about to pull out of UNESCO.

1956 HUNGARIAN REVOLUTION

This is an impressive and very accurate prediction, hardly easy to have foreseen in 1568.

> *Par vie et mort changé regne d'Ongrie,*
> *La loi sera plus aspre que service:*
> *Leur grand cité d'hurlements plaincts et crie,*
> *Castor et Pollux ennemis dans la lice.*
>
> *II.90*

> *Through life and death the rule in Hungary will be changed. The law will become more bitter than servitude. Their great city calls out with howls and laments. Castor and Pollux are enemies in the field.*

The life and death change of Hungarian rule can certainly be defined as occurring during the Revolution of 1956 after Premier Nagy renounced the Warsaw Pact on November 1 of that year and found his country invaded by Russian troops three days later, November 4. History has recorded the strictness of the regime, when many thousands fled to the West and many more were killed or executed. The great city of Budapest was occupied and badly damaged during the fighting. I interpret the last line to mean that pro-Russian Hungarians were fighting against their fellow countrymen (Castor and Pollux were twins). I do not regard it as an astrological manner of dating the quatrain.

TWO ABDICATION QUATRAINS

Pour ne vouloir consentir au divorce,
Qui puis apres sera cogneu indigne,
Le Roi des Isles sera chassé par force
Mis à son lieu que de roi n'aura signe.

X.22

For not wanting to consent to the divorce which will then afterward be recognized as unworthy, the king of the Islands will be forced to flee and one put in his place who had no sign of kingship.

Edward VIII's abdication was not popular among the British people, who had little love for Mrs. Simpson. Edward was therefore forced to leave Britain because of her social standing, "cogneu indigne." Finally George VI, who was not in line for the kingship, is forced to accede to the throne.

Le jeune nay au regne Britannique,
Qu'aura le pere mourant recommandé,
Icelui mort LONOLE donra topique,
Et à son fils le regne demandé.

X.40

The young born to the kingdom of Britain had been recommended to it by his dying father. Once he is dead, London will dispute with him, and the kingdom will be demanded back from the son.

This refers to X.22. Edward VIII is the true heir to the British throne, which was left to him by his dying father. But he will cause scandal (topique) in London by his behavior with Mrs. Simpson, and public hostility toward her earlier divorces caused the king to abdicate, the kingdom taken back from him by the people and given to his brother, George VI.

NIXON

This appears to be a possibly specific description of Nixon and the Watergate bandwagon.

Le grand senat discernera la pompe
A l'un qu'apres sera vaincu chassé,
Ses adherans seront à son de trompe,
Biens publiez ennemis deschassez.

X.76

The great Senate will see the parade for one who afterward will be driven out, vanquished. His followers will be there at the sound of his triumph (a trumpet) their possessions for sale, enemies driven out.

The ex-Senate did dismiss Nixon as predicted and many of his ex-colleagues, now including

Nixon himself, are selling or have sold their "memoirs" to great profits—"possessions for sale." Nixon's social rehabilitation is almost now totally accepted—"his enemies driven out." What a comment upon the morality of American politics, whether Republican or Democrat. It leaves one little faith, Nostradamus or not.

7 THE VATICAN
CONNECTION

One of Nostradamus' greatest fears, identical to those of such modern prophets as the late Edgar Cayce and Jeane Dixon, is based unequivocally upon the vital medieval concept of the millennium. When the year A.D. 1000 approached, everyday life ground to a halt all over Christian Europe. Men ceased to work in the fields, tend their crops or lay up food for the long winter months. Why should they? The Church, the bastion of society as they understood it, had informed them all from every pulpit that the magical number of the year, one thousand years after the birth of Christ, was synonymous with the end of the world. Indeed, it took a good two centuries, well into the twelfth century before man began to comprehend that the inevitable destruction "declared by God" was apparently and definitely not going to happen, and normal social life became reestablished.

But not totally. Unconsciously these threats remained in the minds of the people, particularly the illiterate country folk, but also, surprisingly, were still held by many of the great men of the Church. So as the centuries passed by, the Second Millennium, the year A.D. 2000, grew in importance. The Church could not be wrong a second time. Factors such as the discoveries of the "meanings" of comets in the inevitable cycles of disaster, the predictions of the so-called twelfth-century Irish prophet Malachy, the whole confusion of religious thought of the period, all added to this premonition. This became greatly enhanced when it was realized that a very important comet, the most important since Nexel of 1720 and Kohoutek of 1973/74, would be Halley's due in 1986. This date was close enough to the Second Millennium for the credulous and superstitious, and I, for one, place Nostradamus among this group. He believed it to mark the end of civilization as he knew it, and most of the quatrains dealing with the latter half of the twentieth century are concerned with its malign influence. To Nostradamus the comet was nothing but a harbinger of global disaster: war, famine, pestilence; its influence was understood as wholly malevolent.

As a personal aside I have always wondered at the Catholic Church's dichotomy toward comets. That which announced the arrival of the Christ

Child was a matter of rejoicing. It announced the savior of mankind: or is one being too simplistic? The rest announce disasters.

It is essential that the modern reader understand that the intelligentsia of the sixteenth century regarded the influence of comets as immutable. They believed in their influence for starting or stopping wars, in causing or preventing dynastic marriages and their more general influence upon politics can only be guessed at. The exalted influence of a great comet, visible and unnatural in the heavens, was a fact, not a vague superstition. I am always faintly amused when I think of the so-called Election Comet which appeared on the night of May 9, 1983, when Mrs. Thatcher called her surprise summer election. Perhaps we should still give comets some credence today. She did win, after all.

Although this chapter is essentially concerned with the history of the Vatican during the 1970s–1980s until the coming of the third antichrist, this century is the first time that Nostradamus' quatrains link it also with wars in Africa and the Middle East.

> *De l'Orient viendra la coeur Punique*
> *Facher Hadrie et les hoirs Romulides*
> *Accompagné de la classe Libyque*
> *Temples Mellites et proches isles vuides.*

I.9

> *From the [Middle?] East will come the African heart to trouble Hadrie and the heirs of Romulus. Accom-*

*panied by the Libyan fleet, the temples of Malta and
nearby islands shall be deserted.*

This sounds remarkably pertinent to the troubles
being caused in Northern Africa—Chad, etc.—by
Colonel Qaddafi and his allies from the Middle
East. This last interpretation is made stronger by
the reference to Libya in line three. The "empty
islands" probably refers to Lebanon and its sur-
roundings, ravaged by war for the last twenty years,
and now deserted even by the United Nations
Peace Force.

Nostradamus sees all this as culminating in the
start of a global war by 1986 which shall have its
kernel in the Middle East. One can hardly find this
improbable in present-day politics. Then the third
antichrist appears, or perhaps simultaneously with
the advent of the declaration of World War III (this
is not wholly clear).

Comets apart, and whether we are superstitious
about them or not, it is difficult for the average
modern reader to comprehend the importance of
the papacy in the sixteenth century and all that it
stood for, both spiritually and temporally. Its spiritual powers spread like tentacles into every Christian country; its temporal powers and wealth were
almost beyond comprehension. Neither France nor
the Holy Roman Empire could be considered in the
same league politically. The Vatican was not only
the symbol, it was the entity of religious and mone-

tary power in the Western world at that period. The Moslem world was slowly disintegrating. True, Moslem fleets were still terrorizing the Mediterranean in Nostradamus' lifetime. Ferdinand and Isabella may have conquered Granada in the fifteenth century but the memory of Moorish power in Europe still lingered.

To Nostradamus, therefore, the concept of the decline of the power of the papacy and its implied defilement was truly dreadful. It had little to do with his religious feelings, crypto-Catholic as he may have been by forcible conversion, but a part of his heart lay with the kabala and the secret Hermetic tenets of Judaism. To Nostradamus the final decline of the Vatican was an indication of the end of the old spiritual order as he understood it, and worse, the indication of future anarchy. In short, the end of civilization as he comprehended it.

Some of Nostradamus' predictions about the papacy over these past generations have been proved horribly true. One must remember that for several centuries a papal legate held permanent court at Avignon, and his powers were no less great than those of his titular master. Nostradamus did in fact spend some time at Avignon, at the papal palace, and during that visit concocted what can only be called an aphrodisiac for the papal legate, "the jaded man," which he later printed in his *Traité des fardemens*. Its main interest to the modern mind, and main merit, would seem to be in the costly price of the ingredients. Ground-up pearls and semiprecious stones; perhaps Nostradamus was a more perspicacious psychologist than he is often given credit for? It might certainly help explain the vast fortune he managed to leave on his death. One cannot but think of the various fabulously expensive elixirs of life which tempt the elderly and the rich in our own time.

It is interesting to note that Nostradamus was not greatly impressed with the position taken by Pius XII during the Second World War, and implied that Pius would aid Nazi war criminals to escape from Allied occupied Europe. The prophet actually allied the Pope and Hitler. One cannot but feel that the motto given to Pius XII by the Irish prophet/commentator Malachy on the papacy may have been somewhat ironic—"Pastor Angelicus." Here he allied the Pope with the man of the swastika.

> De la partie de Mammer grand Pontife
> Subjugera les confins du Danube
> Chasser les croix par fer raffe ne riffe,
> Captifz, or, bagues plus de cent mille rubes.
>
> *VI.49*

> *The great Pontiff by the warlike party who will subjugate the borders of the Danube. The crooked cross pursued captives, gold, jewels, more than one hundred thousand rubies.*

The cross is described as "raffe ne riffe," an expression which can mean by hook or by crook, but also by extension, crooked. The crooked cross can only be the swastika. Hitler's party originated in Austria, the Danube. The last line is horribly reminiscent of the millions of pounds of personal jewelry, gold and possessions the Nazis stole from their victims, most of whom ended up in the concentration camps. The position of the Pope in the verse is not clear but Pius XII was criticized for not taking a stronger line against the Nazis and for allowing them refuge in the Vatican City after the war.

It is worth discussing Malachy's prophecies in somewhat more detail. Whether they were known to Nostradamus or not, the two men have many ideas in common. Malachy was an Irishman, reputed to have given a listing of Popes and their mottos from his time, the twelfth century, to the end of the papacy—the Second Millennium. I am of the opinion that the time and dating of the book is the sixteenth century, but since the original text is at the Vatican and not available to general readers this is hard to judge, and how easy it is to be correct in retrospect.

Both Nostradamus and Malachy state there would only be six more Popes after Pius XII, who died in 1958. At the time this seemed extremely unlikely, even considering the average age of an elected Pope. However, following the present Pope only two more remain to come. The attempted assassination of the present Pope maybe will foreshorten even this period. So there seems to be a strong chance that either the Vatican or the papacy itself will have died within the next two decades.

The Pope following Pius XII was John XXIII (1958–1963), whose motto was "Pastor et Nauta," "Pastor and Sailor." Possibly it was this that gave rise to the very amusing and possibly true story that the American Cardinal Spellman, hoping to become the next Pontiff, went sailing down the Tiber with a flock of sheep. However, the man who did succeed John XXIII, Montini, who became Paul VI, certainly did more traveling than any of his predecessors and was greatly influential in the Israeli/Iranian problem and in the Camp David agreement. He had a great influence in the calming of the atmosphere in the Middle East. Interestingly enough, Nostradamus gives John XXIII's coat of arms, which helps to identify him in Century VI, quatrain 20:

> *L'union faincte sera peu de durée*
> *Des uns changés reformés la plus part:*
> *Dans les vaissaux sera gent endurée,*
> *Lors aura Rome un nouveau liepart.*
>
> VI.20

> *The feigned union will last a short time, some changed, the greater part reformed. People will be suffering in the vessels, then when Rome has a new leopard.*

In heraldry a leopard is a lion walking to the left with its head turned left toward the spectator. Pope John XXIII had a leopard in his coat of arms, at a time when it was predicted there would be great changes. There may also be here an oblique reference to the Lions of St Mark. See VI.26.

> *Quand le sepulchre du grand Romain trouvé*
> *Le jour apres sera esleu Pontife:*
> *Du Senat gueres il ne sera prouvé*
> *Empoisonné son sang au sacré scyphe.*

III.65

> *When the tomb of the great Roman is found, a new Pope will be elected the following day: he will not be approved of by the Senate, his blood poisoned in the sacred chalice.*

The dating for this quatrain is found in the first line. A possible "true" tomb of St. Peter had been found in 1979. There is no doubt that the election of Pope John Paul I in the same year was unexpected. Approximately one month after his election he was invited to dine with his Cardinals. He died, unattended, during the night in suspicious circumstances. The ensuing scandal, in European newspapers, did the Vatican no good despite the enormous efforts that were made to hush up the scandal. The facts were that the nuns supposed to attend him at night had been absent for some hours, and his body was cremated, not buried, with suspicious speed. Pope John Paul I was reputed to have been unpopular among his fellow Curia (Senate). When in my earlier book on Nostradamus' prediction of 1971 I mentioned this possibility I was reasonably skeptical. However, I did accept that two attempted assassinations of another contemporary Pope were more probable and the attack on Pope John Paul II has certainly vindicated this in part.

Two other quatrains seem to refer to the "poisoning" of John Paul I.

> *Celui qu'aura gouvert de la grand cappe*
> *Sera induict a quelques patrer.*
> *Les douzes rouges viendront fouiller la nappe*
> *Soubz meutre, meutre se viendra perpetrer.*
>
> *IV.11*

He who shall have the government of the great cloak will be led [toward] execution in several cases. The twelve red ones will come in to spoil the cover: beneath murder, murder will be done.

> *Esleu en Pape, d'esleu sera mocqué*
> *Subit soudain esmeu prompt et timide,*
> *Par trop bon doulz à mourir provocqué,*
> *Crainte estainte la nuit de sa mort guide.*
>
> *X.12*

Elected as Pope he will be mocked by the chosen [Curia] suddenly and unexpectedly removed, prompt and timid. Caused to die, through too much goodness and kindness, he will fear for the guard killed on the night of his death.

The first of these two quatrains seems to imply that had Pope John Paul I been allowed to live he might have ordered changes in the Curia which were serious enough to cause the Cardinals to take prompt action. The reference to the death of the guard in X.12 is unsubstantiated but among all the deliberate obfuscation one has little way of knowing.

An interesting sideline which again drew the world's attention to the influence of Vatican power even in this day and age is the notorious affair of the financial swindling that occurred at the Vatican bank, the Ambrosiana and the consequent scandals relating to the P.2 Lodge in Rome which occurred in 1983. Such dramatic events as the putative "suicide" of Signor Calvi, found hanging under Blackfriars Bridge, his pockets full of brick; the "amazing" escape of the indicted Italian banker from a secure Swiss prison: such events do seem to extend one's credulity. A great deal of power and influence is being exercised behind the scenes. According to a well-known European politician I spoke to recently but who rightly refuses to be named, at the present time the powers exercised by the Vatican are greater than any other in the West, including the United States. Initially this must appear a naive statement, but I think it deserves a certain amount of reflection.

The present Pope, Pope John Paul II, is essentially a Polish political personality, attempting to assert the problems of his nation and those of other U.S.S.R. satellites through his position. His peregrinations are legendary—one almost feels he cannot bear to be constrained for more than a certain time at the Vatican without taking a Papal voyage. After his first attempted assassination in 1981 these are either the acts of a brave or impetuous man. The first attempt took place in the Vatican Square at Rome on May 13, 1981, by the Turk Mehmet Ali Agca. The Pope suffered severe injuries. According to Nostradamus, another attempt will be made, probably in Milan. The Pope made a memorable remark after the first attempt: "Watch your flocks," he counseled, "and be prepared to shed your blood."

The political and other explanations offered by the Italian police after Ali Agca's attempt made little sense when published in 1981. Either one scented total confusion or a cover-up. In October 1983, the Italian, Vatican and Bulgarian (note: not Turkish) police decided to reenact a second attempted murder. Rumors abounded. Agca himself is admittedly a Turk, Eastern enough to fulfill Nostradamus' prediction. But the complexities of his trial involved the Bulgarian Secret Service, particularly one Sergei Antonov, who has been held since November 1982 for suspected involvement in the shooting and is repeatedly stated by Agca to be a key member of the plot, masterminded by the Bulgarians. Little other evidence has resulted to date.

The popular press were less discreet. The recent attempted assassinations of the present Pope are well known. I include below a newspaper excerpt which gives some idea of its impact. It comes from the *Daily Telegraph*, January 8, 1983.

*Turk Stands by Pope Plot Claim—by Leslie
Childe in Rome*

*Italian public prosecutors maintained silence yes-
terday about the outcome of a weekend confrontation between the Turkish hit-man who tried to assassinate the
Pope and a jailed Bulgarian airline official accused of
aiding him.*

*But it is known that Mehmet Ali Agca, who has
reportedly been promised a drastic cut in his life sentence if
he tells police all he knows about the plot stuck to his
"Bulgarian Connection" story.*

*Questions in a heavily guarded room at Rome's
Rebibbia prison lasted several hours. Public prosecutor
Ilario Martella, who is heading the multi-nation investigations into the sensational case, kept firing questions
at both men.*

Denied Everything

*The Bulgarian—Sergei Ivanov Antonov, 34, has
been held in jail since November 25 on a charge of "active
complicity" in the attempt to kill the Pope in St. Peter's
Square.*

*Antonov "desperately denied everything" as the
Turkish terrorist, a member of the "Grey Wolves" once
sentenced to death in his homeland for the murder of a
newspaper editor, gave names and dates. But Agca insisted that Antonov and a Bulgarian Embassy employee,
who has since returned home, were his "pilots" in the plot
to kill the Pope on May 13, 1981.*

He repeated his charge that Antonov was with him in St. Peter's Square when he gravely wounded the Pope.

This interesting report was followed up on the night of May 6, 1983, by a newsflash on the World Service which I heard and recorded myself. It stated that a Portuguese priest had admitted his part in attempting to assassinate Pope John Paul II with a bayonet cut into pieces. However, to my knowledge, this information was never relayed to the press. But Nostradamus' two assassination attempts do appear to have occurred.

Nostradamus incessantly repeats the theme of a disaster which shall reverberate throughout the Vatican and the Church as a whole, occurring at the time of the comet "le grand estoille," therefore clearly not referring either to the poisoning of John Paul I or to the attempted assassinations mentioned above. The prophet seems to envisage that the appearance of the comet will signify two things: either the actual death of the Pope or his "spiritual" death, in which he sees the Holy Father forced to leave Rome itself. Perhaps it is wrong to criticize Pope John Paul's urge to constant travel? He is, however, helping fulfill Nostradamus' predictions to the letter. He is lessening the influence of the papacy at its source through his world-political ambitions and thus possibly starting to diminish the importance of the Vatican itself as the center of the Church. Nostradamus repeats in several quatrains that soon a Pontiff will be forced to leave the Holy

City. These quatrains all seem firmly linked to 1986—to the advent of Halley's Comet. This comet has already been linked to the coming of the Third World War at the time when a Pope named Paul is in the Vatican.

> *La grand estoille par sept jours bruslera,*
> *Nuée fera deux soleils apparoir,*
> *Le gros mastif tout nuict hurlera*
> *Quand grand Pontife changera de terroir.*

> *II.41*

The great star will burn for seven days and the cloud will make the sun appear double. The great mastiff will howl all night long when the great Pontiff changes his abode.

Before discussing this quatrain it is worth linking it with the following:

> *Un peu devant monarque trucidé*
> *Castor, Pollux en nef, astre crinite*
> *L'erain public par terre et mer vuidé*
> *Pise, Ast, Ferrare, Turin terre interdicte.*

> *II.15*

A short while before a king is murdered, Castor and Pollux in the ship, a bearded star. Public treasure emptied on land and sea. Pisa, Asti, Ferrare and Turin are forbidden lands.

Apart from Halley's Comet due in 1986, the only other comet of note at this period is the newly discovered Iras Askari Alcock, one of the largest seen for the last two hundred years. If that is the case, war is nearer even than we think. References to the appearance of an important comet, linked with the destinies of the papacy and the third remaining brother of a powerful American family are also reasonably repetitive. Nostradamus has already described in great detail the assassinations of the two other Kennedy brothers, John F. Kennedy and Robert F. Kennedy. These tragedies will have already occurred by this time, as indeed they have, but the prophet tragically predicts that the third brother, Edward Kennedy, will also be assassinated while never attaining the ultimate position of power. Ten years ago I should have been much less prepared to accept this notion. But now, in his early fifties, lacking the charisma of his two elder brothers, plus personal disasters such as Chapaquiddick and the alcoholism of his former wife—all these events have diminished the man. He does not appear to be the new man of America. Perhaps, even worse, he is the ultimate psychological assassinee?

One of the quatrains that seems to imply the impious power of the third antichrist working deviously behind the scenes long before he makes his ultimate appearance is the following:

> *Les deux unis ne tiendront longuement,*
> *Et dans treize ans au Barbare Satrappe*
> *Au deux costez seront tel perdement*
> *Qu'un benira la Barque et sa cappe.*

> V.78

The two will not remain allied for long: within thirteen years they will have given in to barbarian power. There will be such a loss on both sides that one will bless the barque [of Peter] and the leader.

The major problem of course is to work out who is meant by the two great allies. At the moment it might even imply the United States and the United Kingdom. It certainly cannot imply Russia after the Cuban–Grenada incident and the shooting down of the civilian airliner over Korea in September 1983. China at the moment is unlikely. It is too much involved with trying to reduce its internal crime rate and with the international panics that are beginning to arise over the return of Hong Kong at the end of this century. If the two powers can be read more generally as the U.S.A. or Western Europe then the barbarian power can certainly be interpreted as the Middle Eastern wars. What effect, if any, the intervention of the papacy may have can only be guessed at.

During the course of history, since Nostradamus published in 1568, several Popes have changed their abode. The two most important, both mentioned by him, were Pius VI who died at Valence, a prisoner of Napoleon, and Pius VII who was also forcibly held prisoner in France for a period. But neither of these events was distinguished by the "double sun" of II.41, mentioned earlier. Nostradamus as a scientist was aware of the strange visual effects caused by the gaseous tail of a comet. An ingenious interpretation of the latter is therefore that the sun may appear double through refraction, an optical illusion. Even more intriguing is the fact that the Irish prophet Malachy predicts that the motto of Pope John Paul II will be "de labore solis," of the toils of the sun.

One definitive linking theme of the death of a Pope named Paul, war in Europe and America linked somehow with the fate of the Kennedy brothers is clear enough in the following quatrain:

> *Pol mensolee mourra trois lieus du Rosne* *
> *Fuis les deux prochains tarasc destrois:*
> *Car Mars fera le plus horrible trosne,*
> *De coq et d'Aigle de France, freres trois.*
>
> *VIII.46*

> *Paul the Celibate will die three leagues from Rome, the two nearest flee the oppressed monster, when Mars [war] will take up his terrible throne, the cock and the eagle, France, the three brothers.*

There have been four Pope Pauls since Nostradamus wrote: Paul V—1621, Paul VI 1963–1978, John Paul I—1978 and the present Pope, John Paul II—1978–? The linking with one of the three Kennedy brothers helps to date this quatrain in the near future. A contemporary Pope is predicted to die either just outside of Rome or possibly France if the word Ronse is not a misprint. At this time the two great allies (see V.78) are troubled and threat-

---

*Interpreted generally as misprint for Rome (Rosne).

ened by a dreadful and uncontrollable war. The cock is the normal symbol of France and the eagle that of America, yet another link with the Kennedys. The odds against these factors being linked together four hundred years ago are astronomical—no pun intended!

The next quatrain is somewhat equivocal but it reinforces the link between a comet, the outbreak of the Third World War and the inevitable advent of the third antichrist.

> *Apres grand troche humaine plus grand*
>   *s'appreste*
> *Le grand moteur des siecles renouvelle.*
> *Pluie, sang, laict, famine fer et peste*
> *Au ciel veu feu, courant longue estincelle.*
>
>   *II.46*

> *After great misery for mankind an even greater one approaches as the great cycle of the centuries starts to renew itself. It will rain blood, milk, famine, war and disease. In the sky will be seen fire, dragging a great trail of sparks.*

This is the invariable chorus of war toward the end of a century linked with the appearance of a comet. We must remember for someone such as Nostradamus, educated in the geopolitical ideas of his period, it would be difficult for him to draw the distinction that our generation does between "local" wars, such as Vietnam, Iran, Iraq and Afghanistan, and World Wars because by his standards they

involve vast areas, armies and loss of life. I feel that
all the current wars, especially in the Middle East
and Central America, serve little but to confuse his
sense of timing over this period. And can one
blame him? He is as accurate as his facilities and
comprehension will allow, but the appalling excesses of our modern age are beyond him. That is why
he relies so much on one of the few invariables, the
few absolutes of this period: Halley's Comet. As far
as Nostradamus can comprehend the future of this
world of ours, by the time of the comet's appearance mankind will have gone too far along the path
of disaster to help itself. Global catastrophe will
then be inevitable.

It is suggested that the third antichrist was probably born somewhat over thirty years ago. If one is to
believe him to be a man, and not a creed, this would
make sense. He has probably been groomed for
power for many years and within the next two years
or so will decide when the time is ripe to take action. One of the few specific dates given for his
appearance is December 16, 1986.

> *La grand copie que passera les monts*
> *Saturne en l'Arq tournant du poisson Mars.*
>
> *II.48*

> *The great army will pass over the mountains when
> Saturn is in Sagittarius and Mars moving into Pisces.*

This astrological "square" is very rare. It last occurred in July 1751, and will next appear on De-

cember 16, 1986. This quatrain may not relate to the antichrist—it is only the year 1986 which causes me to make the link. The army is completely unspecified. It could march over mountains from any of the Great Powers, especially China or the U.S.S.R.

To return to our Papal moutons, some past, two to come if both Nostradamus and Malachy are to be believed. Before our present Pope, the personality of John XXIII seemed to attract Nostradamus.

> *Quand ans le siege quelqu'un bien peu tiendra,*
> *Un surviendra libidineux de vie:*
> *Ravenne et Pise, Verrone soustiendront,*
> *Pour eslever la croix du Pape envie.*

VI.26

When for some few years the [Vatican] seat will be held for some small good. The one who succeeds to it is libidinous in life. Ravenna, Pisa and Verona will support him, desirous of elevating the Papal Cross.

John XXIII reigned for approximately four and a half years (1958–63) and was probably a more popular Pope than his successor. Not only did he have the common touch, he also possessed that rare comprehension of human frailties, often lacking in the political celibate. His religious views concerning such subjects as birth control are generally regarded as more liberal and compassionate than those of our present John Paul II, whose deliberate

reversal to many of the older dogmas has caused a
certain amount of crisis in the priesthood.

> *Par le trepas du tres viellart Pontife,*
> *Sera eslue Romain de bon aage.*
> *Qu'il sera dict que le siege debisse,*
> *Et long tiendra et de picquant ouvrage.*

V.56

    *After the death of a very old Pope will be elected
one to Rome of a good age. It will be said of him that he
weakens the [Holy] seat, but he will cling to it with long
and stinging effort.*

This quotation which I take to refer to John Paul
II no longer seems as obscure as when I first read it.
The last line seems a clear reference to the at-
tempted assassination by shooting, and the Pope's
determined and effortful recovery. According to
Malachy the next Pope shall be one characterized
by the word "Olivarius," of the olive branch. But to
Nostradamus' contemporaries this word would
have meant a Benedictine monk. There is only one
Benedictine in the Curia at the present time, the
English Cardinal Basil Hume of Westminster. The
full motto given by Malachy is Gloria Olivetia.
Rumor has it that Cardinal Hume is very popular
among his fellow prelates and his views are regarded as those of a reasonable moderate. If there
were the danger of the outbreak of a global war he
would be an important influence toward world

peace, and a possible candidate for the papacy.

More credence may be given to this view by the argument which broke out on May 9, 1983, between the Cardinal and the influential Monsignor Bruce Kent—a cutting of which I include from that day's *Daily Mail.*

> *Am I in the right church? asks Kent*
> *by John Ryan*
>
> *Cardinal Basil Hume, Archbishop of West-minster, has admitted to "serious misgivings" over Mgr. Kent's role as secretary general of CND, a position he considers might better be filled by a layman.*

It will certainly increase Cardinal Hume's general influence. Mgr. Kent also commented that the present Pope could not be expected to lose the basic influence of his life in Communist Poland, which is reflected for example in his distrust of Latin America. Mgr. Kent's statements seem to be carrying him into a political role outside that of his priestly one. He also stated very clearly that the Pope was not clear in his own mind "between his spiritual and political roles." It seems that maybe here we have two similar personalities albeit from totally different backgrounds.

However, Nostradamus, like all good prophets, does like to leave his options open—I suppose it is an essential part of the "trade," as it were. He quotes a possible reference to a French Pope. However, it is not one of the more convincing of quatrains:

Nul de l'Espaigne mais de l'antique France
Ne sera esleu pour le tremblant nacelle,
A l'ennemi sera faicte fiance,
Qui dans son regne sera peste cruelle.

V.49

Not from Spain but from ancient France will he be
elected for the trembling ship. He will make a promise to
the enemy who will cause great plague during his reign.

Since Nostradamus' day there has never been a French Pope, so this prediction may lie in the future. It indicates that there will be two main candidates for the papacy, one Spanish and one French, when the Church is doing badly, "trembling ship." The French candidate may attempt to be, or even be, elected, and will try to effect a compromise with Communism, with remarkably little success.

Although the Vatican announced the so-called discovery of the true tomb of St. Peter some years ago, according to Nostradamus this has not yet been found, and shall only happen when a great earthquake occurs sometime in the month of April. Perhaps when the San Andreas fault shifts, which is predicted around that time?

Au fondement de la nouvelle secte
Seront les oz du grand Romain trouvés,
Sepulchre en marbre apparoistra couverte,
Terre trembler en Avril, mal enfouetz.

VI.66

At the founding of a new sect the bones of the great

Roman will be found. A sepulcher covered in marble will appear. The earth will quake in April: dreadfully burned.

The sect could refer to Vatican reforms, or on a rather more improbable scale to one of those such as the Moonies which seem to be proliferating in these modern times. There is another reference to an earthquake which occurs on May 14th, but unfortunately Nostradamus gives us no hint as to the year.

This next quatrain is more imaginative. I feel that the anagram Medusine, converting to Deus in Me, is a typical Nostradamus pun.

> *Roi exposé parfaira l'hecatombe*
> *Apres avoir trouvé son origine*
> *Torrent ouvrir de marbe et plomb la tombe*
> *D'un grand Romain d'enseigne Medusine.*

> *IX.84*

> *The king will complete the slaughter once he has found his origin. A torrent to open the tomb of marble and lead, of a great Roman with the Medusine device.*

The key to this lies in the word Medusine. If it really is an anagram of "Deus in Me," this would indicate that the tomb was the true resting place of St. Peter, as that was his emblem.

8 THE DAWNING CRESCENT

Nostradamus has a habit, as I imagine do most predictors who write as much material as he did, of repeating certain themes with a monotonous regularity, as though trying to stress their importance to the reader, particularly through verbal tricks such as his use of "trigger" words.

One of his most insistent themes is that of the overthrow of the Shah of Persia (unimaginable when I wrote of that glorious feast he gave in the desert to celebrate his wedding to his third wife, Farah Dibah) by a man who would sit plotting against him in Paris. This man, the man of white, the man of the White Turban, living in France, would return to inflict an era of cruelty upon Persia quite incomprehensible to the West. He in his turn will then be removed from power by a mysterious figure designated only as "Perse," the man of blue, the Persian. Two other names are linked with that of Perse, but they remain as yet unclear, Alus and Mabus. However they are similar enough to possibly indicate the same individual and according to Nostradamus their intentions toward the world are wholeheartedly evil. These names are either an amalgam of that of the antichrist or of disciples of Perse. Somehow these personalities may nurture and educate the antichrist as Nostradamus understands him. And it is this final creature who will originate the Third World War, the devastation of which is beyond even the prophet's descriptive ability.

It has only been in the past two or three years that I have begun to perceive in the Prophecies an inexorable link which appears to lead toward the end of civilization as we know it, unless some great power (Nostradamus' Allies?) stands up not only against its force but against its propaganda. I personally believe in free will but unless it is exercised by those in a position of influence, soon, calmly and deliberately I cannot but foresee the imminent doom of mankind, a wasteland where we shall find no salvation, for there will be none. I have often been accused of being a pessimist; perhaps people who interest themselves in prophets, in men of "doom and gloom," usually are.

It is important to remember that I, as a translator and tentative interpreter of the *Prophecies* cannot possibly *know* if Nostradamus will be proved correct or not in the future. What he has written that has been accurate in the past is astounding, but he has made mistakes as well. After all, he did write over four hundred years ago. Technically he should score about five "bull's eyes" out of 4000. His average, according to the "credibility reading" of various computers I have used, varies between 50 and 70 percent. They can offer no explanation for this, any more than I can.

Facing the situation of world power politics as I saw it writing in November 1983, I find that the apparent lack of balance, and therefore judgment in some of our world leaders is quite terrifying. It reduces me and many of the people with whom I have discussed it, to a state of near fatalism. A poll was held among school children in November 1984 in England, and of these 28% believed nuclear war would kill them and another 45% that their lives won't be affected by it. If this causes depression and fear in children so young the future generation has little to look towards. Let us hope that if this book is ever published the world will have got over these particular crises. Sometimes one feels the only solution is a cosmic miracle: Halley's Comet perhaps? The only fly in this particular ointment is that Nostradamus' vision of the future must be compared with, say, a huge colored panoramic cinema screen as opposed to a small black and white television set. He foresees our future on that sort of scale. I indicate in chapter 9 how frequently this has been the case. However, I do hope the little that I

do comprehend of his visions may be of some relevance. Whether anyone can achieve a positive result so near to Doomsday is another question.

Nostradamus' comprehension of the third antichrist is ambiguous. I feel that he envisages a forerunner—a John the Baptist, as it were—whom he
names the "Perse" who initially opens the paths to
world-wide destruction. There is also the faint possibility—and in my own interpretations I do stress
faint—that the third antichrist is himself not a person but a philosophy. However, a philosophical
concept so deadly to mankind that it makes Marxism look like the Salvation Army does not seem
likely. Nostradamus has always looked upon the
third antichrist as a person in the quatrains, not an
ideology.

The situation in the Middle East during the
"eighth decade" i.e., the 1980s, has always been
regarded by Nostradamus as being of vital importance. He envisaged the way this epoch was han-
dled as being the possible trigger for a Third World
War. There have been so many wars both in the
Middle East and North Africa over the last ten
years that it is almost impossible to conceive when
Nostradamus suddenly considers them as becoming of the utmost danger to us all. Colonel Qaddafi,
the PLO, the Ayatollah, the assassination of President Sadat of Egypt, the tragic events in Lebanon,
Israel, Ethiopia, Afghanistan and Chad. Are these
not list enough? Now we are faced with the tragic
killings of French and American soldiers in

Lebanon, part of the International Peace Force, and the continuous maintenance of the American presence in the area with warships and aircraft. The *Guardian* newspaper in Britain in its headline for October 23, 1983 was quite unambiguous: "The West Is Involved in War with the Middle East." Where will it all end?

The first specific reference to "Perse" in the *Prophecies* is the one that intimates clearly that he will annihilate the regime of the Ayatollah as thoroughly as the latter did to the late Shah.

> *La teste bleu fera la teste blanche*
> *Autant de mal que France a faict leur bien,*
> *Mort à l'anthene grand pendu sus la branche*
> *Quand prins des siens le Roy dira combien.*
>
> *II.2*

The blue head [leader] will inflict upon the white one as much damage as France did them good. Death from the great antennae hanging from the branch, when the king will ask how many of his men have been captured.

It is not unreasonable to link the white leader with the Ayatollah Khomeini; partly because both he and his followers affect it as the color of their headdress, even more so, those fanatics who have adopted the white shirt of the martyr to his cause, which indicates that they will fight to the death for their beliefs in a Holy War. This white leader is then indicated as being overcome by a blue one, who shall reduce Iran to an even worse state than it is in at present. Perhaps he is to be found in Iraq?

Certainly the Ayatollah has come into his own. He is now one of the centers of world unrest, the absolutist head of a bloody régime.

> *Plui, faim, guerre en Perse non cessée,*
> *La foi trop grand trahira le monarque:*
> *Par la finie, en Gaule commencée,*
> *Secret augure pour à un estre parque.*

I.70

> *Rain, famine and war will not cease in Persia. Too great a trust will betray its monarch. These actions, started in France, will end there, a secret sign for one to be sparing.*

This is certainly one of Nostradamus' least ambiguous predictions. Perse then continues to extend his ambitions and achieve them, in the Middle East, in Egypt and Greece he causes great bloodshed. The assassination of Sadat and the reign of the Colonels were reasonably contemporaneous events.

> *Par feu et armes non loing de la marnegro,*
> *Viendra de Perse occuper Trebisonde*
> *Trembler Phatos Methelin, Sol alegro,*
> *De sang Arabe d'Adrie couvert onde.*

V.27

> *With fire and weapons, not far from the Black Sea will he come, from Perse, to occupy Trebisonde. Phatos and Mytilene tremble, the Sun is bright, the Adriatic sea covered with Arab blood.*

Dans Foix entrez Roy ceiulee Turbao,
Et regnera moins revolu Saturne,
Roi Turban blanc Bisance coeur ban,
Sol, Mars, Mercure pres de la hurne.

IX.73

A king enters Foix wearing a blue turban, he will reign for less than a revolution of Saturn. The King with the white Turban, his heart is banished to Byzantium: Sun, Mars and Mercury near Aquarius.

Accepting that these two figures are again Perse and the Ayatollah, the quatrain makes it clear that the "reign" of Perse is considerably less than the duration of one of Saturn's revolutions, that is, twenty-nine and a half years. Unfortunately we are given no idea how long it will actually last. The date indicated by this plan is probably February 18 but the year is not clear. But what world politician would have predicted the Shah's predicament in 1978 or believe it to be a fact that it was written down by 1568? Facts cannot be altered in this sense. The Ayatollah devoted his life to the downfall of the Pahlavi family and succeeded. The last line of the quatrain is somewhat obscure. Although in one sense the new Iran is extremely Spartan in concept, it is more than generous in its letting of blood. It is cruel, extreme and retrograde.

The Shah's exile and death in Egypt seem to be foretold in the following:

Des grands d'entre eux pas exile esgarés
Par teste perse Bisance fort pressee.

V.86

Some of the great men among them wander in exile. Byzantium [Turkey] is hard pressed by the leader of Persia.

According to Nostradamus, the Ayatollah's reign dissolves rather suddenly into a confused end, partly due to Russian interference, the oil crisis, and the final arrival on the scene of Perse. Russian influence is possibly indicated here, and possibly Iraq.

La Loi Moricque on verra defaillir,
Apres un autre beaucoup plus seductive:
Boristhenes premier viendra faillir,
Par dons et langue une plus attractive.

III.95

The Moorish law will be seen to fail, followed by another that is more pleasing. The Dneiper will be the first to give way through gifts and tongues, to another more appealing.

Does this indicate the end of Islamic law as we now understand it, hopefully to be followed by a less harsh régime? But it is difficult to comprehend what Nostradamus may mean by Russia giving way to another through gifts and appealing words. The failure of the Islamic law could, however, be related to another very specific prediction concerning the

State of Israel at the end of the twentieth century—
the century of the sun.

> *Nouvelle loi terre neuve occuper,*
> *Vers la Syrie, Judee et Palestine:*
> *Le grand Empire, barbare corruer,*
> *Avant que Phoebus son siecle determine.*

III.97

A new law will occupy a newly created land,
around Syria, Judea and Palestine. The great barbarian
Empire falls into decay, before the cycle of the Sun is
completed.

As I have said, this age of Aquarius is also the
century of the Sun. Could this quatrain indicate
Israel's ultimate victory in her territories? Geographically no other country has been artificially
created "around Syria, Judea and Palestine" in this
century. One might also remember Nostradamus'
covert but definite Jewish background.

Referring back to Russia's extraordinary change
in policies (III.95), this may be caused by the influence of Perse, or for fear of weapons built up, according to Nostradamus, both in the East and the
West. Perse is at the moment a complete enigma.
He must, if he is to obtain power so soon, be at least
thirty years of age, no stripling or political puppet
will wield such powers. He appears to be a man of
consuming ambition, another Hitler, and one without whom the world would be a better place.

I must at this point indicate some of the contradictions and confusions in datings that appear in the *Prophecies* concerning the arrival of Perse and the consequent dating of the coming Third World War. I suppose Nostradamus cannot be blamed for the confusion; with contradictory reports that appear daily in our contemporary media, he may sometimes have truly just not been able to understand twentieth-century political motives. Sometimes he seems certain that the U.S.S.R. will ally with the West against the Asian antichrist.

> *Par deux fois hault, par deux fois mis à bas*
> *L'orient aussi l'occident foiblera,*
> *Son adversaire apres plusiers combats*
> *Par mer chassé au besoign faillira.*
>
> VIII.59

> *Twice put up and twice cast down the East will also weaken the West. Its adversary, after several battles, chased at sea, will fail in time of need.*

Here we have two major powers at war with each other, and then allied against a third adversary. This will be preceded by world famine. Since the world has lived with this concept for so many generations it is not much help as a dating factor, except for the fact that famine in this overpopulated century is worse than it has ever been. The problems in the countries bordering on the Sahara, Ethiopia, Chad, Mali, and even now the once rich lands of the Cameroons and Zambia spring immediately to mind. When the two powers join in the alliance, it is but short lived. Victory lies in the West.

> *La regne à deux laissé bien peu tiendront*
> *Trois ans sept mois passés feront la guerre.*
> *Les deux vestales contre rebelleront,*
> *Victor puis nay en Armorique terre.*

IV.95

    The rule left to two they will hold it a very short time. Three years and seven months having passed they will go to war. The two vassal [countries] will rebel against them. The victor then born on American soil.

Clearly the two great powers who join in alliance hold ascendancy for a very short while. After three years and seven months of wasted diplomacy they will declare war. It is worth speculating whether Amorique—America—is the third power or one of the original allies. I cannot find any indication as to which the vassal powers might be. However, the line referring to America does seem to mitigate some of the harm indicated in the previous quatrain (VIII.59). To be absolutely clear, it must be stated that in sixteenth-century French the word Armorique was an archaic usage for the northern state of French Brittany. However, such a meaning is most unlikely in this context and I feel Nostradamus' usual "phonetic" interpretation of the word to mean America is here quite acceptable.

According to the *Prophecies*, as the power links between the two allies grow stronger they are reported to the "man of blood," the antichrist.

> *Un jour seront desmis les deux grands maistres,*
> *Leur grand pouvoir se verra augmenté:*
> *La terre neuf sera en ses hauts estres,*
> *Au sanguinaire, le nombre racompté.*

II.89

> *One day the two great powers shall be friendly. Their great might shall be seen to expand. The New Land shall be at the height of its powers. To the man of blood the number (troops, weapons?) is reported back.*

This seems to declare very clearly that when America, "Terre Neuf," will be in a state of world dominance, through means of which one may approve or not, we return to the old conundrum. Which is the other Allied power and to whom does the allegiance of the "man of blood" belong?

After November 1983, when President Reagan sent a huge fleet into the Middle East and his fighter planes actually made so-called "reconnaissance" sorties over strictly Syrian territory, it is easy to read many obvious factors into this. Would it not be ironic if Reagan's self-assurance made him into the "homme sanguinaire"? He is obviously right to resent the deaths of the American soldiers of the International Peace Force in Lebanon, the apparently totally unjustified shooting down of the Korean civilian airliner and the Marxist-Cuban régime sitting so close in Grenada, yet alone Yasser

Arafat's desperate stand between two rebellious factions of the PLO in Tripoli, but one does get the terrible feeling that his lack of political subtlety may well lead us to the brink, if not beyond, of chaos.

A clue as to the probable sign of the "man of blood" as not being American may be found in IV.50, where his origin is given as Asiatic.

> *Libra verra regner les Hesperies,*
> *De ciel et terre tenir la monarchie:*
> *D'Asie forces nul ne verra peries,*
> *Que sept ne tiennent par rang la hierarchie.*

IV.50

> *Libra will be seen to reign in the West, holding rule over the skies and the earth. No person shall see the strength of Asia destroyed, until seven shall have held the hierarchy in succession.*

This last line is a dating. The speed with which Chinese heads of power have succeeded each other since the death of Chairman Mao should offer us no comfort. Jiang Quing's political group, when indicted, were known as the Gang of Four. We now have a new leader, Deng Xiaoping so there is very little time left to us if Nostradamus is to be believed. When Libra, the Balance, rules in America it shall appear all powerful, as it does at the moment. But once the seventh Chinese comes to power, this force will start to decline. All the reader has to do now is come to some sort of terms with the monster who follows in the wake of these catastrophes, the final destroyer, the third antichrist.

9 THE THIRD ANTICHRIST

The advent of the Third World War, according to Nostradamus, will be heralded by an attack upon New York—city and state—through both bombs and chemical warfare.

> *Cinq et quarante degrés ciel bruslera,*
> *Feu approcher de la grand cité neufve,*
> *Instant grand flamme esparse sautera . . .*
>
> *VI.97*

> *The sky will burn at 45 degrees. Fire approaches the great new city. Immediately huge, scattered flame leaps up . . .*

The state of New York lies between the 40th and 45th parallel in the U.S.A. Here is a staggering coincidence. The attack appears to be very widespread, covering both the state and the new city, and the scattered flame may well be that of a nuclear holocaust.

> *Jardin du monde au pres de cite neufve,*
> *Dans le chemin des montaignes cavees,*
> *Sera saisi et plongé dans la Cuve*
> *Beuvant par force eaux soulfre envenimees.*

X.49

> *Garden of the world, near the new city, in the road of the hollow mountains. It will be seized and plunged in the tank, forced to drink water poisoned with sulphur.*

When I first translated this quatrain I assumed, rather simplistically, that the water supply of New York City would be poisoned; whether by sulphur or some more sophisticated chemical it was impossible to tell. Nostradamus' vocabulary was not capable of our twentieth-century distinctions. But when it was disclosed in November 1983 that unclean water tainted with radioactivity had been leaked from Harrisburg, Pennsylvania, the "garden of the world," since 1979 and possibly for as much as eight years earlier, it does give one some cause for thought. Harrisburg is only 180 miles from New York City. Three Mile Island administrators have a great deal to answer for if only in fulfilling the predictions of a man who wrote four hundred years earlier.

The "Cuve," which literally means a huge tank, I interpret as the nuclear reactor at Harrisburg where the contaminated water was initially stored. I also love the description of New York as the "road of hollow mountains." What could be closer to a city of skyscrapers?

There is a strange quatrain in Century II which may be one of the guides to the ambiguous name of the antichrist who follows upon "Perse," although it is hard to decipher with any clarity.

> *Le penultiesme du surnom du prophete*
> *Prendra Diane pour son jour et repos:*
> *Loing vaguera par frenetique teste*
> *Et deliverant un grand peuple d'impos.*
>
> II.28

> *The last but one of the prophets' name will take Monday for his day of rest. He will wander far in his madness, delivering a great nation from subjection [taxation?].*

This certainly seems to imply a non-Christian leader, presumably Moslem or Asian, whose name shall begin with one of the penultimate names of the Prophet, normally spelled Mahomet or Mohammed. I do not understand the reference to the Holy Day as being a Monday. It belongs to none of the major religions as we know them. Whether he is the antichrist to come or a forerunner is not clear.

This quatrain does, however, lead into two fascinating possibilities as to the name of the third antichrist of Nostradamus' Prophecies. Once he is named as Alus, in the second as Mabus, such an easy corruption of the Latin Malus: the Evil One:

> *Mabus puis tost alors mourra, viendra,*
> *De gens et bestes une horrible defaite:*
> *Puis tout à coup la vengeance on verra*
> *Cent, main, soif, faim, quand courra la comete.*
>
> II.62

> *Mabus will soon die and then there will be dreadful destruction of people and animals. Suddenly vengeance will be revealed, a hundred to hand, thirst and hunger when the comet will pass.*

The usual Nostradamus dating of Halley's Comet, 1986, is probable in this context, even if only that it fits in with so many of the other predictions, particularly those in the chapter on the papacy. Is Mabus/Alus an anagram of the name of the third antichrist? As a successful physician Nostradamus knew full well that diseases which kill both animals and man are almost unknown. I discount the plague in this case because I believe he would not call rats "animals." I am afraid the gift of Alus/Mabus may well be nuclear—fallout perhaps? So all we can do is await the arrival of the comet and its consequent "horrible defaite." The only other quatrain one can relate to these is the one which refers to the "bloody Alus," "Alus Sanguinaire."

> *Sa main dernier par Alus sanguinaire*
> *Ne se pourra par la mer guarantir:*

Entre deux fleuves craindre main militaire
Le noir l'ireux le fera repentir.

VI.33

His hand finally through the bloody Alus, he will be unable to protect himself by sea. Between two rivers he will fear the military hand, the black and angry one shall make him repent his actions.

Nostradamus does use the trigger word "main," hand, with both these figures. I don't suppose a finger on a button meant much to him, but few people in the twentieth century would doubt its meaning: the control of the nuclear strike—whether it be Cruise missiles, Pershing II or the Russian Intercontinental missiles, SS20s. Many of the letters I have received over the past two years have suggested that the "hand on the button" is that of President Reagan. It did not seem very probable initially. Since November 1983 I must revise my thoughts. If this is the case, the American president is also inextricably linked in some way with the third antichrist. Even if he gets to serve another term, as seems likely, he probably will not complete it. Civilization, as we know and understand it, will have been wiped from the face of the earth.

There is an unpleasant quatrain which may describe the Cruise missile agreement at this time:

Le chef de Londres par regne l'Americh,
L'isle d'Ecosse tempiera par gellee

Roi Reb auront un si faux anti christ
Que les mettra trestous dans la meslée.

X.66

The London Premier, through American power
will burden the island of Scotland with a cold thing.
"Polar." Roi Reb will suffer so dreadful an antichrist and
will bring them all into trouble.

The deployment of the Cruise missiles is certainly not limited to Greenham Common. There are bases deployed in Scotland and all over the country for both Cruise and Pershing II missiles. One almost feels that the last missiles ever to be fired would be those on Greenham Common. It is a political diversion from basic facts: brilliant propaganda. But to be fair to Nostradamus, he may have been thinking of Polaris, "the cold thing" installed by Harold Macmillan. One fact that troubles me greatly is the number of people who have contacted me to say that they believe "Roy Reb" is some form of anagram for President Reagan. I cannot see this in Nostradamus' vocabulary, but, stranger things than this have happened so I can but leave an open but skeptical mind upon this point. He was, after all, an actor in Western movies. But the missiles are also deployed in many other places over Britain. I make no political comment. I just find it so extraordinary that Nostradamus could even envisage these "rockets of destruction in the sky."

Nostradamus certainly sees a strong link between the ending of the papacy and religious feeling in the world as he understood it. Apart from the "liberal political" Christianity of South America this does appear to be the situation at the present.

> *Du Pont Euxine et la grand Tartarie,*
> *Un roi sera qui viendra voir la Gaule*
> *Transpercera Alane et l'Armenie,*
> *Et dans Bisance lairra sanglante Gaule.*

V.54

> *From beyond the Black Sea and Great Tartary there will be a king who will come to see France. He will pass through Alanica and America and leave his bloody rod in Byzantium.*

Cryptic as always, this quatrain is certain that the man will come from beyond Tartary, Russia. The Alanians, in the division of Tartary, which roughly covered the whole of Central Asia, were situated to the north of the Caucasus and the Armenians to the south. Nostradamus presumably sees the "king," or conquerer, passing through Persia down to the Balkans. Beyond Tartary, there remains only Asia. A similar mention of a man with "a bloody rod" connected with France occurs in II.29. Perhaps the rod is a weapon of some sort rather than the actual wielding of power? This leads to the unambivalent crescendo of the following.

> *Tant attendu ne reviendra jamais*
> *Dedans l'Europe; en Asie apparoistra*
> *Un de la ligue islu du grand Hermes,*
> *Et sur tous rois des orientz croistra.*

X.75

Long awaited he will never return in Europe, but he shall appear in Asia. One of the league issued from the great Hermes, he will grow above all other powers in the Orient.

This could be another reference to Perse or the antichrist himself. In terms of the Hermetic literature Hermes stands for Jupiter and Mercury which generally means Islam. The two other antichrists were European, Napoleon and Hitler. But there is no question but that this third antichrist will definitely arise in Asia. This theory seems extraordinary but one cannot at least accuse Nostradamus of inconsistency. A possible sign of the Third Coming is probably already around us in the fates of the Middle East, Afghanistan, Kurdistan, Ethiopia, Chad, and of Lebanon.

> *Sur le combat des grans chevaux legiers*
> *On criera le grand croissant confond*
> *De nuict tuer monts, habits de bergiers*
> *Abismes rouges dans le fossé profond.*

VII.7

When occurs the battle of the great light horse it will be claimed that the great crescent is destroyed. To kill by night, in the mountains dressed in shepherd's clothing, red gulfs in the deep ditch.

The crescent again confuses the reader because it is essentially a Moslem emblem.

A possible dating for the beginning of the war is given in astrological terms in the following complex quatrain.

Faulx à l'estang joint vers le Sagitaire,
En son hault AUGE de l'exaltation.
Pest, famine, mort de main militaire,
La siecle approche de renouvation.

I.16

When a scythe joined with a pond in Sagittarius is at its highest ascendant. Plague, famine, death from military hands. The century approaches its renewal.

I am inclined to interpret the word "scythe" as containing two meanings: the obvious astrological one of Saturn, but also the metaphorical one of the Russian system, as seen in the hammer and sickle. The pond stands for Aquarius. Therefore, if Nostradamus is to be believed, when Saturn is in conjunction with Sagittarius in the ascendant, we should expect a great war with the usual concomitants of disease and famine. However, the Prophet is not entirely correct in this forecast. Aquarius can never be in conjunction with Sagittarius. Saturn "exalted" in the sign of Aquarius only occurs in the signs of Cancer (June/July), Pisces (October/November) or Scorpio (February/March). Saturn moves into a Water sign every seven years. Perhaps the scythe is an obscure prediction of the Russian sickle, Marxism?

Another more specific prediction gives the date of the war as 1995.

Chef d'Aries, Jupiter et Saturne,
Dieu eternel, quelles mutations?
Puis par long siecle son maling temps retourne

Gaule et Italie, quelles emotions?

I.51

At the head of Aries, Jupiter and Saturn: eternal God what changes? Then the bad times return after a long century: what turmoil in France and Italy?

As I mentioned, the last conjunction between Jupiter, Saturn and Aries occurred on December 13, 1702, and the next one is predicted for September 2, 1995. But this brings back echoes of the old dilemma of the millennium, and as I have already stated, Nostradamus seems unclear as to the dates of the war—from the end of 1986 to 1999—a span of thirteen years.

A series of earthquakes, occurring more frequently than in the past, shall also be another indication of what is to come. There will be one dreadful one on May 14—we are not given the year, but it is reasonable to assume it will be before 1986.

> *Sol vingt de Taurus si fort terre trembler.*
> *Le grand theatre rempli ruinera,*
> *L'air ciel et terre obscurcir et troubler*
> *Lors l'infidelle Dieu et sainctz voguera.*

IX.83

When the sun is in twenty degrees of Taurus there will be an earthquake. The great city [theater] full of people, will be shattered. Darkness and trouble in the air, on sky and land, when the infidel ignores God and the saints.

Many readers interpret this quatrain as referring to the San Andreas Fault, in California, where another shifting of the earth's crust is long overdue. "Sol vingt de Taurus" means quite simply twenty days after the sun moves into the zodiac sign of Taurus, which would be May 10. The reference to the times being no longer truly Christian probably helps to place the quatrain in this century.

Experts on the world's internal turmoil and shifts are trying to establish whether scattered earthquakes which have killed more than 6000 in 1983 alone are in any way related as a large convulsive pattern. None of the experts can really agree but the debate has certainly thrown up more torment for those living in California. Those scientists who link earthquakes with the motions of the moon say that a few years "on either side" of 1987 "at times near full or new moon and near sunrise or sunset, one might be more likely than otherwise to observe one or more larger earthquakes in California." Cheerful reading. How could Nostradamus possibly have guessed? The new land of America was still almost an unknown quantity, but there it is, in black and white. One seismologist told me that the shocks from a really severe quake in California would definitely be felt as far away as New York.

What I personally call Nostradamus' "millennium dating", I feel is more superstition than knowledge, despite Mrs. Dixon's convictions to the contrary.

L'an mil neuf cens nonante neuf sept mois,
Du ciel viendra un grand Roi deffraieur.
Rescusciter le grand Roi d'Angolmois.
Avant que Mars regner par bonheur.

X.72

In the year 1999 and seven months from the sky
will come the Great King of Terror. He will bring back the
Great King of the Mongols. Both before and after this,
war reigns unrestrained.

I think the last line is the most important here.
Whether the Asian King of the Mongols is to appear as late as 1999, war will have been widespread
for some years. Perse, Alus, Mabus, or all three?

Even after the turn of the century there seems
little hope for the human race—such of it that sur-
vives.

Apres grand troche humaine plus grand
*   s'appreste,*
Le grand moteur des Siecles renouvelle.
Pluie, sang, laict, famine fer et peste,
Au feu ciel veu courant longue estincelle.

II.46

After great misery for mankind an even greater
approaches when the great engine of the Centuries is renewed. It will rain blood, milk, famine, war and disease.
In the sky will be seen a fire, dragging a tail of sparks.

As I have constantly reiterated in the chapter on
the papacy in particular, comets were of immense

value in helping date events, particularly those in the future, and to confirm their solemnity. So it does seem possible that line 4 of the last quatrain refers as always to Halley's Comet of 1986. However, the raining of blood and milk is very ominous. After Hiroshima great black blobs of rain fell for days on the contaminated cities. And what is this appalling misery mankind experiences even before the great engine of the centuries is renewed? A very disturbing quatrain.

The influence, if not the man himself—the third antichrist—is always presumed by Nostradamus to have been behind the assassination of the two Kennedy brothers, John F. Kennedy and Robert. He also implies very clearly that Edward Kennedy will meet the same fate, but that his position will never be that of power attained by his brothers.

> *L'AntiChrist trois bien tost annichilez*
> *Vingt et sept ans durera sa guerre.*
> *Les heretiques mortz, captifs, exhilez.*
> *Sang, corps humain, eau rougi gresler terre.*
>
> *VIII.77*

> *Antichrist will very soon annihilate the three, his war having lasted some twenty-seven years. The unbelievers are dead, captive, exiled; blood, human bodies, a trail of red water spattering the earth.*

There is an intriguing "double" meaning in the first line of the quatrain. Three separate antichrists are definitely described in Nostradamus' epistle to the Prophecies. But equally, it is the third antichrist who annihilates the "three." It is difficult to find any other group of three in this century, after Hitler, in power and known world-wide, other than the Kennedy brothers, two of whom have already been assassinated who fit this description. Tragic although it may appear, it does seem that Edward Kennedy, despite his "low profile" since the scandal of Chappaquiddick, is a psychological possibility. Whether this war of twenty-seven years should be related to those which have dragged on for so long in the Middle East and Africa, yet alone Vietnam, can only be a matter of conjecture. Equally, maybe it will take approximately twenty-seven years before the world will become comparatively safe after a nuclear holocaust. There is a definite emphasis toward Africa—a new development.

> *Le Monde proche du dernier periode,*
> *Saturne encor tard sera de retour:*
> *Translat empire devers nation Brodde . . .*
>
> *III.92*

> *The world is nearing its final period. Saturn will again be late on his return. The empire will shift toward a black [Brodde] nation . . .*

"Brodde" in Ancien Provençal meant black or dark brown: does this quatrain deal with the future of the African nations, now so involved politically with both East and West? It also contains the lesser meaning of decadent. Possibly the use of the word empire could refer to the infamous reigns of either Idi Amin of Uganda or that of the Emperor Ange Patasse Bokassa, whose excesses during his coronation surpassed even those of Napoleon. There is always a faint chance that Zimbabwe may be referred to.

The general picture portrayed by Nostradamus is that initially two great powers will ally against a third, but this friendship shall sadly be of short duration. Although at the moment it is geopolitically almost incredible that the Allies will be the U.S.A. and the U.S.S.R., the constant references to an Eastern antichrist make it more feasible.

> *Quant ceux du polle artiq unis ensemble,*
> *En Orient grand effrayeur et crainte:*
> *Esleu nouveau, soustenu le grand tremble*
> *Rhodes, Bisance, de sang Barbare taincte.*

> VI.21

> *When the people of the northern pole are united together, in the East will be great fear and dread. A new leader is elected, supported by a great one who trembles. Rhodes, Byzantium will be stained with barbarian blood.*

But we should not fear too much. The theme is continued more strongly and a victor declared.

> *La regne à deux laissé bien peu tiendront*
> *Trois ans sept mois passés feront la guerre.*
> *Les deux vestales contre eux rebelleront,*
> *Victor puis nay en Amorique terre.*

> IV.95

The rule left to two, they shall hold it a very short time. After three years and seven months have passed they will [have to] go to war. Two vassals will rebel against them: the victor then born on American soil.

If this continues the reference to the Allies in the former quatrain, world peace will only last for three years and seven months after which they are forced to take some form of warlike stance; "feront." Who the vassal countries are is impossible to say. But victory finally lies in the West, with America.

It is at this point that the world must take note. The theme of the two great Allies is again repeated, but again the "man of blood" is introduced.

Un jour seront demis les deux grands maistres,
Leur grand pouvoir se verra augmenté.
La terre neuf sera en ses hauts estres
Au sanguinaire le nombre racompté.

II.89

One day the two great leaders shall become friends. Their great power shall be seen to grow. The new land will be at the height of its power: to the man of blood the number is reported.

The key to this quatrain lies in the word "demis" in line one. It is almost certainly a misprint for d'amis, which I have used. To understand demis in its usual sense of hatred, would make nonsense of the rest. Powers of great leaders cannot be increased if they are halved. Line three seems to link the two powers with America again. The problem for the modern reader is this: when does Nostradamus' "man of blood" consider himself and his rival to be at the height of their powers and a danger to both himself and his beliefs?

The present building up of Cruise missiles, Pershing IIs, etc., does not seem to bode well for the West. Nostradamus implies that our arms build up is so great, so committed perhaps, that the West will force the East into a warlike position. This could well be the case.

> *L'horrible guerre qu'en l'occident s'apreste*
> *L'an ensuivant viendra la pestilence,*
> *Si fort horrible, que jeune, vieux ne beste,*
> *Sang, feu, Mercure, Mars, Jupiter en France.*
>
> *IX.55*

> *The dreadful war is being prepared in the West, the following year will be followed by the pestilence: so very horrible that young, nor old nor animal [will survive] blood, fire, Mercury, Mars, Jupiter in France.*

I have a horrid fear that the pestilience, covering so many victims will again be nuclear fallout.

One cannot but feel that Nostradamus' vision of the twentieth century was one of war, brutality, famine and disaster. Equally, as must be so often repeated, prophets are of essence men of doom and gloom, and one cannot expect the rhapsodies of a self-deluded world savior from such a character. This is an extremely unsettling chapter and is intended to be read as such. Perhaps even now some men of power, in whose hands lies the fate of the world, might just pause for a short while and consider where their present inexorable policies are leading us.

10 OTHER RECENT PROPHETS

If one is to believe J. W. Dunne, a faculty for precognition is by no means unusual, implying that many people have the ability to make prophecies, but comparatively few actually use their gift. No doubt some see it as a burden, best avoided. Most of what Dunne has to say relates to precognition in dreams, or in free association when in a waking state. His interests were largely confined to prediction on a small scale, about private events in the relatively near future, most of which could not readily be subjected to independent verification. In this chapter about other recent prophets I shall exclude all short-term, small-scale private domain prophecies, not from any lack of belief in them, but because it seems to me that an examination of longer-term, larger-scale public domain prophecies should provide more compelling evidence of the existence of valid prophecies to the skeptical reader.

The word "recent" in the title of this chapter will be interpreted liberally, to include all prophecies about recent and near future identifiable occurrences, even if they were made hundreds of years ago. Some of the prophets or sources of predictions are, of course, still alive.

It seems necessary to make a distinction between predictions that are in some sense inspired and those that are derived from rational calculations of immediately relevant data. The distinction is easier to make in practice than it is to justify by some kind of watertight theory. Thus I venture to doubt whether so urbane a character as General Sir John Hackett would claim that his somewhat frightening *History of the Third World War, August 1985,* was inspired. In contrast, the series of prophecies made by Edgar Cayce and Jeane Dixon are quite clearly inspired, even involuntary. George Orwell's *1984* has captured the public imagination so much that its title and some of its concepts have become a part of our language and culture. Though in part inspired, it is also based firmly on experience and hence better classified among the calculated prophecies.

Essentially, Orwell made one big prophecy, about the existence of a particular way of life in one country by a certain time. Aldous Huxley's *Brave New World* and H. G. Wells' *Things to Come* were similar portmanteau prophecies, the former more inspired than the latter.

Purely economic forecasts about such things as the rate of growth in industrialized countries, being derived from close analysis of economic statistics, obviously have no place in this chapter. Perhaps room should be found for F. A. von Hayek's *Road to Serfdom* which, being anti-socialist, has not captured the public imagination, though it now appears to be a much better prophecy than when it first appeared forty years ago. Neither do dizzying works of relatively general prophecies, such as those by Toynbee, Spengler, Pareto and Marx, and the almost annual predictions that capitalism is entering its final crisis, have any place in this chapter.

I have also excluded recent founders and organizers of independent religions or sects such as the Mormons, Rastafarians, Seventh Day Adventists. At least in the eyes of their followers, such religions and sects are based on revelations, which to my mind are different in character from inspired prophecies.

The ability to prophesy on the grand scale is, in my view, very rare indeed. It seems appropriate then, to start with the "inspired" prophets before going on to the "rational" calculators, though of course these categories should not be taken to be mutually exclusive.

Inspired prophets make relatively large numbers of predictions over a long period of time, which are gathered together by themselves or others in book form. As a rule no large-scale organization of their thoughts is apparent. Contrast that with the predictions by rational calculators whose usual preferred form is the novel, written by themselves. Most of those discussed here are professional writers who have written one or more predictive novels. H. G. Wells wrote several, Aldous Huxley one, George Orwell one, Sir John Hackett one; Andrei Amalrik used the essay.

THE INSPIRED PROPHETS

In his *Patterns of Prophecy,* published in England in 1974, Alan Vaughan provides an English translation from a German original printing of 1848 of some prophecies said to have been made by a Polish monk in 1790. They include:

—1938, when a universal war in the whole world in which man against man will be intent only on death, will draw all creation into destruction. Interpretation— The Second World War.

—In the year 1986 once again peace will be established; it will be only a few years. The end of Gulf Wars, but according to Nostradamus the flash point of the Third World War.

—In 1988 a terrible comet will appear in the heavens. This is obviously a reference to Halley's Comet; like the first prediction just slightly wrong in the actual dating.

—In 1996 a universal earthquake will shake the whole earth, and all Italy, Sicily, Portugal and Spain will vanish forever into the ground. Could this be the great earthquake that Nostradamus envisages for America—the shifting of the San Andreas fault? But again, the two men differ on dates.

—Finally there comes in the year 2000 the last day of the Lord, on which he judges the living and the dead. The traditional millennium.

Most of these look to me like a slight rearrangement of Nostradamus' predictions and may therefore not be from an independent source. I also have some reservations about the authenticity of the prophecies of Malachy, at least in the sense of doubting that they really go back earlier than the sixteenth century.

The prophet Malachy is said to have been born in Ireland in 1094 or 1095, and to have made prophecies about the popes who would rule up to about the year 2000. The prophecies are very brief, only three or four Latin words for each pope, which may relate to his name, coat of arms, background, personal characteristics or events in his reign. Some believe that the prophecies of Malachy were fabricated in the middle of the sixteenth century, or even in the nineteenth century. At least that allows the authenticity of the prophecies relating to the ten most recent popes. For those since 1939 we have:

Pius XII	1939–1958	An angelic shepherd
John XXIII	1958–1963	Pastor and mariner
Paul VI	1963–1978	Flower of flowers
John Paul I	1978	Of the half moon
John Paul II	1978–	From the toil of the sun (or) of the eclipse of the sun.

There are left for the future "The glory of the olive" and "Peter the Roman," after whom comes the last judgment and the destruction of Rome.

A pope may choose his coat of arms to fit the prophecy, unless the cardinals have already chosen a pope who fits it. Papal elections can make prophecies self-fulfilling, a rather ill-known fact. The important thing about Malachy is his prediction of an approaching end of the papacy, something that he has in common with Nostradamus. As I have already mentioned, at the time of the 1958 conclave there was a rumor in Rome that the American Cardinal Spellman cruised up the River Tiber with a boat full of sheep. Pastor and mariner. Prophecies should not be taken too literally, I feel.

Edgar Cayce (1877–1945) was primarily a healer, only secondarily a prophet, and most of his prophecies were of personal rather than public events. He made many predictions about earthquakes and other earth changes, mostly without specific dates. He believed in an endless cycle of life, and that he himself had had previous lives, memories of which he could reach only occasionally. One might call him a living example of a sentence which appears at the end of *Clea*, the fourth novel of Lawrence Durrell's *Alexandria Quartet*: "Time is memory they say; the art however is to revive it and yet avoid remembering."

Cayce made all his predictions, or readings, in a trancelike state akin to sleep. Questions were put to him, which he answered, but he was unable to recollect his answers when once more in a waking state. Throughout his life a devout Christian, he was an undoubted mystic, in touch as he saw it with some kind of universal mind, akin to the collective unconscious of C. G. Jung, whom Cayce never read. Two important things differentiate him from other mediums, prophets, shamans or other people "possessed" in some way, whether Christian or of any other religion. First that he was always himself in trance, never possessed by a specific ghost or spirit. Secondly, that he usually spoke intelligible English in his trance readings, using other languages (of which he had no waking knowledge) when one or other of them was appropriate to the person seeking a reading or to the questions being put to him.

To give more than two readings a day was too much of a strain on his health, something he had in common with other genuine mystics of all ages. Personal presence of the person seeking a trance reading was not necessary, especially for his medical diagnoses. These he could do equally well if instructed in trance by his wife or secretary to examine the body of such and such a person at a given address. His diagnoses were usually followed by cures, often unorthodox, but frequently successful. To avoid the hostility of the medical profession, Cayce worked as an unofficial aide to certain doctors, or referred patients to osteopaths and physiotherapists as well as doctors.

He predicted 1936 as the beginning of a period of upheavals and wars; that was the year in which the Spanish Civil War, often seen as a prologue to, or the first act of the Second World War, broke out; the prediction was made in 1932. He foresaw 1929 as the beginning of the Great Depression, and 1933 as the beginning of the recovery. In 1939 he predicted that the U.S.A. would be at war in 1941, and in 1941 that the Second World War would end in 1945 or 1946. (His ideas on a religious rebirth in Russia are not too far from those of Solzhenitsyn and Amalrik.) Some of his "World Events" predictions were comparatively lacking in specific time and place details and therefore, like some of Nostradamus' predictions, not easy to verify. But for Cayce that was unimportant in comparison with his real life purpose as a healer.

In 1956, eleven years after the death of Edgar Cayce, the Association of Research and Enlightenment bought back his former hospital and re-opened the vaults, containing some fifteen thousand of his trance readings, whose analysis continues.

Louis Hamon, using the pseudonym Cheiro,

wrote *Cheiro's World Predictions,* published in London in 1927 and *Cheiro's World Prophecies,* published in 1931. These books included a prophecy that England and France would be at war with Italy and Germany, another that London would be partly destroyed by Russian airplanes. He predicted severe earthquakes in the coming fifty to one hundred years, particularly in various parts of the American continent and around the Azores in the North Atlantic. He also predicted civil war in Ireland, the coming freedom of India and its partition, the expansion of Palestine by the Israelites, war between the U.S.A. and Japan, and a coming Age of Wars. He could be described as half inspired, half calculating.

The American Jeane Dixon is probably the most well-known of contemporary prophets of the inspired kind alive in the Western world. Though she differs in many ways from the late Edgar Cayce, they have one very important thing in common, a profound belief in the Christian religion. Mrs. Dixon claims that her precognitive experiences come to her in several different ways, including revelation direct from God, telepathic communication, dreams, interpersonal vibrations, in response to prayer, visions while gazing into a crystal ball, psychic visions in response to objects. She has an impressive record of predictions that have already come true, in both the private and the public areas of activity.

Mrs. Dixon's life is much more public than that

of Edgar Cayce, and her healing powers are not as great as his. She has sometimes been able to predict the winners of horse races and to provide stock market forecasts. Her use of multiple methods for receiving guidance presents an interesting contrast with the single method (the trance) used by Cayce; she is aware of the messages that she has received, whereas he had to be told what he had said in trance. I believe in this she is unique.

As long ago as 1948 Mrs. Dixon had visions of race riots in the U.S.A., apparently organized by Soviet Russian agents, which would continue into 1968 and beyond. That there were race riots is a matter of published historic fact. Eleven years before the assassination of President Kennedy, Mrs. Dixon predicted that a Democrat would be elected President of the U.S.A. in 1960 and that he would be murdered while in office.

By 1960, Mrs. Dixon predicted the assassination of Martin Luther King, Jr. in 1968, the year in which he actually was killed. She believed that by then he would no longer be useful to the Communist elements in the National Association for the Advancement of Colored People (NAACP), and that they would therefore arrange for him to be killed. She had further warnings of the assassination shortly before the event, and after it a psychic vision of a small group of people working out the details of the planned assassination.

In her book *My Life and Prophecies,* Mrs. Dixon writes that she wanted a friend "to persuade President Kennedy not to make that fateful trip to Dallas, yet I realize now my efforts were pointless because his death was shown to me in a revelation, and a revelation of destiny can never be changed." There is an interesting implication here, that it may be possible to evade the dangers shown precognitively in other ways. Mrs. Dixon has a quite different view of another death that she predicted. Quoting again from her book, "When RFK died, it was not because he had to die. His life could have been longer and more productive—yet he chose to die. . . . all of the visions I received about the pending death of Senator Robert F. Kennedy were reflections of thoughts of men. Men planned his death, not God." Mrs. Dixon was able to predict even the place of the assassination, and made repeated attempts to meet the Senator or to get warnings to him in other ways.

Mrs. Dixon's other successful predictions include the partition of India, the assassination of Mahatma Gandhi, the Communist takeover in China, the death of Dag Hammarskjöld. Among her predictions for the future are:

> —a comet striking the earth in the middle
>   of the 1980s
> —tremendous war in 1999
> —drastic changes in the Catholic Church
> —peace in Ireland "as soon as the influence
>   of certain American, self-righteous
>   groups is eliminated"

—Chinese invasion of the Middle East in
the year 2000
—a woman President of the U.S.A.
—Russia once more Christian (the latter
strikes one as particularly unlikely, but all
prophets are victims of wishful thinking,
Nostradamus among them.)

The Comet prediction is obvious. The course of
Halley's Comet was mathematically forecast many
years ago. I think that the war in 1999 is pure
medievalism—the millennium yet again rearing its
ugly head. The third is probable, except that at the
moment the Vatican's politics and statements of belief are retrograde; however the new Marxist-Cath-
olic priests of the Third World counterbalance this.
The fourth statement is ambiguous. It has been
well known for many years how strongly parts of
the United States have supported the I.R.A. I dismiss the Chinese invasion as being confused again
with the millennium, and think it will occur, if it
does, somewhat earlier. Mrs. Geraldine Ferraro
made the faint hope of a woman President of the
United States a possibility. And, as I say, for the
last, I cannot foresee, even in the most practical
way, that the U.S.S.R. will revert to Christianity.

Predictions of the assassination of President Kennedy in 1963 could draw on a long history of deaths
in office, by violence or from natural causes, including every president from 1840 elected or reelected
in a year divisible by twenty. Presidents Harrison,

Harding, Roosevelt died from illness. Presidents Lincoln, Garfield, McKinley, Kennedy were assassinated during their terms of office. President Reagan was elected in 1980 and again in 1984. I am not making a prediction, merely drawing attention to a well-known pattern of events.

THE RATIONAL PROPHETS

H. G. Wells combined an admirable ability for technological and social prediction and foresight combined with a total lack of personal political competence or awareness, which is revealed in particular in his meeting with Stalin in 1934. His description of the dictator as a modest diffident sort of man whom no one feared was equaled only by the monumental naiveté of his fellow-Fabians, Sidney and Beatrice Webb, in their *Soviet Communism, A New Civilisation?* A year before his death in 1946, Wells may have sensed his political folly without wishing to admit it even to himself; it was in 1945 that he wrote *Mind at the End of Its Tether*, with its bleak message that the end of life on earth as we know it was at hand. Wells had a tendency to identify the universe with himself—his death would be the end of everything. He was not, therefore, a true prophet in the normal sense, who would see events after their death.

But when he died he had fifty years of prediction behind him, from *The Time Machine* of 1895, before

Einstein, in which time is a fourth dimension of space. Given that, why should one not be able to travel in time? The Time Traveller does exactly that by designing machines, the first on a small scale and the second large enough to contain himself, which can go into the past or the future simply by accelerating objective time, though the precise methods of doing that are not made clear. The rate of change of velocity of time can be controlled, to avoid the difficulties of attempting to occupy the same space-time position as some other object. His first voyage was brief; he did not return from the second. Wells could not foretell what he should have foreseen and took the easy novelist's way out.

It was the first of many novels of science and technology in the future, followed by *The War of the Worlds* (1898), *The First Men in the Moon* (1901), *Anticipations* (1901) and *The War in the Air* (1908). *Anticipations* described what life would be like a century later foreseeing special roads, the enormous growth of motor trucks, motor omnibuses, and privately owned motor carriages; urban diffusion and expanding suburbia; continual growth of the middle classes of society; the virtual disappearance of domestic servants; and the appearance of a successful airplane, before 1950! A short story of 1903, "The Land Ironclads," portrayed tank warfare in the near future; but Leonardo da Vinci centuries earlier had visualized such machines. In *War in the Air*, just five years after the Wright brothers' first flight, Wells puts forward the idea that airplanes will bring about a profound change in the character of warfare, which will become an affair of areas rather than fronts, and more importantly, profound changes in its consequences; wars would be more destructive and less decisive. These books were more prophetic than the earlier, better known ones.

The World Set Free was published in 1914. Wells predicted the discovery of atomic disintegration leading to transmutation in 1933, something actually achieved in 1934, and the dropping of the first atomic bomb in 1958, which actually happened in 1945. Given Wells' method of rational calculation rather than inspiration, it would be unfair to criticize him for poor timing. His politically naive side showed in 1914 with his belief that it was "The war that will end war," after which it would be easy to set up a Peace League to control the world. Not surprisingly, he disliked the League of Nations that was set up in 1920, unable to see that political possibilities always conditioned and limited the search for vast general solutions.

The Shape of Things to Come, his most considerable work of prophecy, was published in 1933; a film version, produced by Alexander Korda, came out in 1936.

In the book, using the time theories of J. W. Dunne, an official of the League of Nations managed to obtain the text of a history book written one hundred and fifty years later. It related how war broke out in 1939 in consequence of a quarrel over Danzig between Poland and Germany—in itself a very successful prediction. The world is reduced to ruins, from which there ironically emerges one group with a sense of purpose, the airmen responsible for the destruction. They impose order on mankind, bring about a world state, and begin the long rebuilding process. Human nature is legislated out of existence; religion, culture, leisure and sport forbidden or frowned upon. In time the élite master genetic engineering and many other techniques.

By 1939, with *The Fate of Homo Sapiens*, Wells was losing faith in the future. He saw the war as ending in the collapse of civilization, a repetition of 1914–1919 on a much greater scale. Nothing but disordered barbarism could follow. The way was set for *Mind at the End of Its Tether*.

Aldous Huxley projected *Brave New World* six hundred years in the future. It was first published in 1932. The calendar has become, instead of A.D., A.F., meaning After Ford, though in the records of the culturally-deprived society then existing there is confusion between Henry Ford and Sigmund Freud, an amusing light touch in what I feel to be an otherwise rather unsympathetic work. There had been a war in about A.F. 150, during which biological rather than nuclear weapons had led to the imminence of total destruction. Total control of human beings, a rigid hierarchic society, and world government were the necessary means of avoiding that. Huxley wrote a new Foreword to an edition published in 1946:

". . . it looks as though Utopia were far closer to us than anyone, only fifteen years ago, could have imagined. Then, I projected it six hundred years into the future. Today it seems quite possible that the horror may be upon us within a single century. That is, if we refrain from blowing ourselves to smithereens in the interval . . . . we have only two alternatives . . . either a number of national, militarised totalitarianisms . . . or else one supra-national totalitarianism . . . developing, under the need for efficiency and stability, into the welfare-tyranny of Utopia."

One cannot give Huxley marks for success on particular prophecies when the whole thing is set so far in the future, though now fifty years after the book was written his scientific and technological predictions look in large measure to be much nearer in time than he first thought. The Bakanovsky process, which can produce many thousands of persons from one human ovary, the manufacture of human beings by mass-production techniques into predetermined castes in carefully calculated ratios, Pavlovian methods of conditioning infants, what one would now call subliminal methods of teaching during sleep, the Feelies at the cinema adding tactile sensation to sight and sound, all appear within the measurable range of present-day technological research and achievement. All these processes are leading toward the de-humanization of man, and artificial insemination and "rent-a-womb" show us to be following fast in Huxley's footsteps.

Cultural interests such as reading Shakespeare, long-lasting sexual love, the family, even the wish to spend time alone, are things to be discouraged and prevented lest they encourage independent thought, which is virtually equivalent to subversive action. In Orwell's *1984,* the ruling apparatus has the same hostility to human sexual love and privacy. The motto of the World State is "Community, Identity, Stability," more reminiscent of the "Travail, Famille, Patrie" to be found on French coins during 1941 to 1944 than of the resounding "Liberté, Egalité, Fraternité" to be found on them before and after the German occupation of France.

Henry Ford's "History is Bunk" is an implicit motto. Only the higher castes are permitted to know anything about it, because for them it serves to emphasize the pleasures, and of course responsibilities, of their privileged positions. War, want, old age, disease, pain, insecurity, religion have been abolished for all members of society, whatever their caste; conditioning has ensured that no one feels discontented by unequal treatment.

I detect in the new caste of the KGB and their families in the Soviet Union some similarities to the Alpha-Pluses of *Brave New World;* they have many privileges, all must obey them, within limits they may think their own thoughts. Imagine the combination of a KGB sort of hereditary ruling class and a caste system on Hindu lines. It could happen in much of Asia, Europe and Africa. *Brave New World* may yet prove to be good prediction in some parts of the world. And I have met many scientists and mathematicians who would genuinely welcome such a society in England, seeing themselves of course in the rôle of Alpha-Pluses. They are welcome to it.

Andrei Amalrik, a Soviet dissident who emigrated to the West in 1976, wrote his essay, "Will the Soviet Union Survive Until 1984?" in 1969. It was first published in English in 1970. A new edition with other essays was published in 1980, but without significant changes in the title essay, which is a conscious echo of George Orwell's date. It is clearly a work derived from rational calculation rather than from some kind of inspiration. He quotes in the preface to the 1980 English edition from the Russian poet Vladimir Solovyov, writing in 1894:

> O Rus! Forget thy former glory,
> The double-headed eagle's smashed,
> Thy banners given torn and tattered
> As play things to the yellow children.

That could be taken as a prediction of the conquest of Russia by the Chinese. In his essay Amalrik writes: ". . . we may point to the period between 1975 and 1980 for the beginning of the war between the Soviet Union and China."

In his Preface Amalrik still holds a wildly exaggerated and very outdated opinion of the power of "the Soviet Union, a slowly dying yet still monstrously powerful colossus capable of crushing the whole of Europe in the palm of one hand." In the late nineteenth and early twentieth centuries, European statesmen occupied themselves with the problems of "The Sick Man of Europe," that is, how to cope with the consequences of the disintegration of the Turkish Empire. A hundred years later, I believe that there is a new "Sick Man of Europe," the Russian Empire. Amalrik puts a specific timing, but it is, in my opinion too early:

> . . . the collapse of the régime will occur some time between 1980 and 1985 . . . I have no doubt that this great Eastern Slav empire . . . has entered the last decades of its existence. Just as the adoption of Christianity postponed the fall of the Roman Empire but did not prevent its inevitable end, so Marxist doctrine has delayed the break-up of the Russian Empire—the third Rome—but it does not possess the power to prevent it.

Writing on *Detente and Democracy in 1976,* Amalrik stated his belief that various developments would delay disintegration several years beyond 1984. Writing in 1977 in *The Movement for Human Rights in the USSR,* Amalrik wrote that "in the West, both left and right-wing politicians, interested above all in the status quo, take an unfavorable view of the Movement for Human Rights in the USSR." It seems that the Soviet Union is already a Sick Man. One does not need to think of the tragic farce of President Andropov's turn in power, nor even to speculate on the present régime of 1985.

General Sir John Hackett was born in Australia in 1910. After a distinguished career in the Army he became Principal of Kings' College, London, and later visiting Professor of Classics, a subject he studied at Oxford. He is editor and principal author of *The Third World War, August 1985. A Future History.* The first edition was published in 1978, the second in 1982; very likely there will be further revisions.

In his book, the Soviet Union invades Yugoslavia to support a rebellion, American troops intervene to protect the innocent victim state, and general war follows. In the first edition, it is all over in a few weeks. The initial tacit agreement to avoid the use of nuclear weapons is broken by the nuclear destruction of Birmingham, England, swiftly followed by the destruction of Minsk, capital of the Byelorussian Republic. That sets off a coup d'état in the U.S.S.R. by a Ukrainian KGB general, who had obviously learned from Beria's mistakes and was practical enough to kill off the President of the U.S.S.R. and the head of the KGB before taking power in the Politburo. A hotline call to the President of the U.S.A., and peace comes in a few hours.

The whole book is interesting, not in my judgments to be taken as a prophecy of what will happen, but more as a cautionary tale of what could go wrong if NATO were not strong and resolute. I disagree with some of the political judgments, in particular Hackett's seeming to take Soviet intentions or designs as realistic: I am far from sure that the Soviet leaders are sufficiently competent, or that their economy has the necessary resources to effectively underwrite these global aspirations. The enemy is more naive than we think. When Hackett writes that the U.S. "Think Tanks Report on the Poor South, November 1984," it seems to me wrong in many ways, though I am not sure whether the author is expressing his own opinions or the undue simplicity that might be expected in such a report. It is all us or them, left or right; Asia, Africa and Latin America do not neatly follow simple North Atlantic categories. China may not have an economic miracle, South Africa will not disintegrate, Jamaica, Zimbabwe and Egypt probably will not be run by unstable left-wing aggressive régimes. I seem to be putting my own political prophecies against those of Sir John Hackett and his team, which is not the point of this book. However, when we met on television in Dublin some years ago, we seemed remarkably in accord.

GEORGE ORWELL AND 1984

One can summarize the prophetic novels of Wells, Huxley and Orwell by saying that the first two were of Utopian societies, more or less desirable, whereas the third was the practical vision, from below, of a humanitarian. Orwell believed that *Brave New World* and *Things to Come* bore far less relation to future political reality than Jack London's *Iron*

Heel, a novel about a Communist or Fascist dictatorship written some thirty years earlier.

No one could accuse George Orwell of political naiveté. He fought on the Republican side in the Spanish Civil War, yet was able as early as 1937 to see more than a passing resemblance between Stalinism on the one hand and Fascism on the other, using the strange jargon of those days where "Fascism" meant German National Socialism plus Italian Fascism plus the Nationalists and Falangists in Spain. By 1938 he was back in England. Unlike many left-wing intellectuals, he supported the war against Hitler from its outbreak in September 1939. He took Hitler seriously, in contrast to Wells who looked on him as a joke; he took Stalin seriously too. By 1943 at the latest he was aware that totalitarianism was more likely to grow than to contract after the end of the war, and he has been proven all too right.

Animal Farm seems to have been in his mind by 1938, but was not written until the winter of 1943–1944. It is not a work of prophecy, more a satire on past and present realities in the Soviet Union, with recognizable portraits of Marx, Lenin, Trotsky, Stalin and Molotov among the ruling pigs. Perhaps to avoid offending the Soviet leaders, it was not published until the war ended in August 1945. *1984,* his single major work of prophecy, was being planned before he started writing *Animal Farm.* The book was completed by the end of 1948 and was published in June 1949. Within a year of publication it had sold over 400,000 copies, but by then Orwell was dead at the age of 46. Huxley's major prophetic work looked six hundred years ahead, Nostradamus four hundred years, that of Wells one hundred and fifty years, and Orwell's just thirty-six years into the future. The time scale was shortening. Utopia whether for good or evil was getting nearer, now this side of the millennium that some prophets see as so dangerous.

1984 has itself become a word in our language, along with "doublethink" (the capacity to simultaneously accept and believe in two contradictory explanations or theories), "newspeak" (the official language in *1984*), "prole" for member of the proletariat, and "Big Brother is watching you." The action of the novel takes place in 1984, in England which is part of Oceania, one of the three superstates engaged in a perpetual power struggle; the other two are Eurasia and Eastasia. The ideological creed of Oceania is "Ingsoc," meaning English Socialism. The language is continually being simplified and purged of dangerous words, with the sublime objective of making it impossible to express disloyal opinions or even have disloyal thoughts. It is not clear whether this debasement of language extends to the upper ranks of the Party, who do not appear in *1984*.

The principal character of the novel—"hero" would be the wrong word for him—is Winston Smith, born in 1945, who works at the Ministry of Truth, on whose façade one finds the three slogans of the Party:

WAR IS PEACE
FREEDOM IS SLAVERY
IGNORANCE IS STRENGTH

In Smith's youth an atomic bomb had dropped on Colchester, and ever since then Oceania had been allied with Eurasia against Eastasia, or vice versa. Since the late 1950s there had been no external records to which to refer. Winston's job, along with many other people, was to continuously revise all newspapers and books so that they always agreed with the latest Party instructions on what had happened. Every apartment had a tele screen, at once a television receiver and transmitter, which had to be on at all times, so that "they" could watch you. Unknown Thought Police circulated everywhere. People vanished without trace, and the lists on which their names had appeared were revised as though they had never existed. Tragic shades of the late Argentinian régime. Every day on the tele screen there were organized Hate Sessions for the Enemy, Goldstein, always present, always foiled, but never destroyed.

Only Inner Party members had the right to turn off their tele screens and be private for a while, say half an hour. Winston Smith begins to keep a diary, starts a love affair with Julia and commits thought crimes by conspiring against the Party with an Inner Party member and by reading Goldstein's book. Soon Smith and Julia are arrested by the Thought Police, of course "betrayed" by the Inner Party member. He is beaten, interrogated, tortured until he is prepared to accept that $2 + 2 = 4$ or 5 or 3, even all of these, if that is what the Party says.

Finally, Smith collapses, telling the Inner Party member to torture Julia, not him. After his release, they meet. Smith and Julia have each betrayed the other. The novel ends with Smith knowing that he really loves Big Brother, a sort of Stalin figure and that he has returned to what he was—a non-person.

Of the three super-states, Oceania is most of America plus the British Empire; Eurasia is Russia plus Continental Europe; Eastasia is China, Japan and Southeast Asia. All of that is not very good political prophecy. Orwell's vision is of what England will have become by 1984, not all at once, but over a period of about twenty-five years. The rest of Oceania must be similar, for Ingsoc is the ideology of the whole super-state; nothing is known of the ideologies of the other two super-states. In fact, something like Ingsoc is the ideology only of the Soviet Union, China and certain of their satellite states.

Yet there are other parts of the world where some of the features of life in Oceania have been or are true. Not so long ago many people disappeared without trace in Argentina. There are one-party states in Africa whose party guidebooks contain references to the Enemy, against whom party militants must be perpetually on their guard. There are countries in several parts of the world whose governments dislike independent newspapers, or newspapers of any kind in some cases; in them, "hostilepress" is one word, for how can anything permanent be anything but hostile? Rewriting of newspapers and books may not be so far away. One sees in many places new constructions very soon falling to pieces, from bad design and inadequate maintenance, escalators no longer working at all; La Défense in Paris is one such place, already reminiscent of *1984*. The word "fascist" is continually used as a mindless term of abuse by progressive intellectuals in Western countries, reminiscent of the hate campaign against the enemy Goldstein in *1984*. Deviationists in the Soviet Union are tormented to restore their "sanity," just as in *1984*, usually through hospitalization and the use of mind-bending drugs.

Was Orwell writing a prophetic book, or a grim warning of how awful the future could be if the wrong choices were made? In some ways *1984* can be seen as similar to Wells' *Mind at the End of its Tether*, both deeply pessimistic works written when the authors were nearing the end of their lives.

1984 was also the year chosen by Jack London in *The Iron Heel* (1906) for the completion of the wonder-city of Asgard by millions of wretched serfs, the people of the abyss, after fifty-two years of effort. I do not know whether that is anything more than coincidence. The form of *The Iron Heel* is that of a twentieth-century narrative, with annotations written in the twenty-seventh century. Attempts at socialist revolution in 1912–1913 were crushed, followed by three hundred years of the Iron Heel (a ruthless dictatorship) and four hundred years of the Brotherhood of Man (socialism). There was no experience of socialism in 1906, so that London could sincerely believe that dictatorship and socialism were opposed rather than identical.

The Shape of Things to Come and *Brave New World* are views of society from above, from the upper ranks of the Inner Party, in Orwellean terms. Nothing is said of such exalted persons in *1984*, where the view is from below. Orwell's proles are not too different from Huxley's "Epsilon Semi-Morons," and the Inner Party member O'Brien would be at most a Beta Minus. Perhaps all three books are different points of view of rather similar social organisms—a frightening vision, but is it a true one of the future?

Prophecy and prediction of both the inspired and rational calculated kinds on the larger stage of political events are very much alive and will continue, for all their uncertainties, so long as we can avoid choosing or accepting totalitarian forms of government that place meaningless ideals above human beings.

11 MISUSES OF PROPHECY AND PROPHETS

One of the most prevalent misuses of prophecy is the faking of texts or altered words, which must go back at least to the time of the Greek oracles. There have been many editions of Nostradamus containing interpolated or altered quatrains. It took me all of seven years to get hold of a copy of the first complete edition of 1568, to be quite sure of working from an authentic text; my copy, incidentally, at one time belonged to the Society of Jesus, or the Jesuits. So far as I know, most other recent interpreters of Nostradamus have admitted to using seventeenth-century editions, which contained many corruptions in the text and several false quatrains. This is true of even the better of them, for example Edgar Leoni and James Laver. I have preferred in this chapter to write in terms of "misuse" rather than abuse, so as to include involuntary as well as deliberate actions.

The texts of Nostradamus, in particular, have suffered much misuse over the last four hundred years, by interested parties trying to force meanings that were not there, for good or evil purposes, by the deliberate changing of words, lines or whole quatrains, and from wilfull misunderstanding by the emotionally credulous. Since prophets have been misused from exploitation by others for material gain or political advantage and from being persecuted or understood too well or insufficiently, certainly the fact that some prophets have not really believed in their predictions should, in my opinion, be counted as a form of misuse.

Macbeth is a classic example of one of the most frequent misuses of prophecy, that of trying to force it instead of just letting it happen. As the Third Witch says in Act I, Scene III:

> *All hail, Macbeth, that shalt be king hereafter!*

and a little later, to Banquo:

> *Thou shalt get kings, though thou be none.*

Banquo remains doubtful:

> *And often times, to win us to our harm,*
> *The instruments of darkness tell us truths,*
> *Win us with honest trifles, to betray us*
> *In deepest consequence.*

Soon enough Macbeth murders the king, to

make one of the prophecies come true. Banquo speaks to Macbeth in Act III, Scene I:

> *Thou hast it now: King, Cawdor, Glamis, all*
> *May they not be my oracles as well,*
> *And set me up in hope?*

In Act III, Scene III Macbeth has Banquo murdered, presumably to prevent the other prophecy from coming true. Banquo's son escapes from the murderers. Macbeth still hungers for more prophecy:

> *And betimes I will, to the weird sisters:*
> *More shall they speak, for now I am bent to*
>   *know,*
> *By the worst means, the worst.*

During his second encounter with the witches Macbeth hears three prophetic sayings:

> *. . . beware Macduff!*
> *. . . none of woman born shall harm Macbeth.*
> *Macbeth shall never vanquish'd be until*
> *Great Birnam wood to high Dunsinane hill*
> *Shall come against him.*

and sees a vision of a line of eight kings, descendants of Banquo. From then until his death Macbeth believes in prophecy, becoming almost its passive agent, and demonstrating another misuse of prophecy, that of wrongful interpretation, in the way most favorable to himself. When the second and third prophetic sayings come true, in a sense unfavorable to him, Macbeth's courage fails, and he is killed by Macduff. It is overstating the obvious that at least 50 percent of a prophecy's content lies in belief by its subject.

Contrast the conduct of Macbeth with the advice given by Galadriel to those using her Mirror of the future in Tolkien's *Lord of the Rings*.

At the bottom, on a low pedestal carved like a branching tree, stood a basin of silver, wide and shallow, and beside it stood a silver ewer.

With water from the stream Galadriel filled the basin to the brim, and breathed on it, and when the water was still again she spoke "Here is the Mirror of Galadriel," she said. "I have brought you here so that you may look in it, if you will . . ."

"What shall we look for, and what shall we see?" . . . *"What you will see, if you leave the Mirror free to work, I cannot tell. For it shows things that were, and things that are, and things that yet may be. But which it is that he sees, even the wisest cannot always tell . . . Some never come to be, unless those that behold the visions turn aside from their path to prevent them. The Mirror is dangerous as a guide of deeds."*

The important message is at the end. By trying to prevent an unfavorable prophecy from coming to pass, you may in fact unintentionally work to bring about its fulfillment. It seems to me that the principle of symmetry demands that someone trying to ensure that a favorable prophecy should come to pass, will in fact help to ensure that it fails. That was Macbeth's error. Prophecies should illuminate one's actions rather than determine them with the exception of warnings of disasters. To ignore this fact is to invite danger.

The first misuse of Nostradamus' name by a living person occurred very soon after his death. Jaubert, Nostradamus' first biographer after his pupil de Chavigny, writes of his so-called eldest son Michael—known as Michel le jeune. In fact as we know from his will, Nostradamus had three sons and three daughters: the sons were César, who was described by Pitton in 1666 (*Histoire de la ville d'Aix*) as "a good poet, excellent painter and able historian." He is also registered as being Consul for Salon in 1598 and 1614. The second was André, who went to Paris soon after Nostradamus' death and was arrested for killing a man in a duel. It is said that he vowed to take Holy Orders if released and duly became a member of the Capucines and is reputed to be buried at the Monastery at Brignoles near Toulon. The third, Charles, was a Provençal poet.

Michel le jeune, as it is most convenient to call him as he was no relative of Nostradamus, used several other pseudonyms, notably that of Antoine Crespin Nostradamus. Under this name in 1571 he published a pamphlet interpreting a recent earthquake. As Michel le jeune, various writings are attributed to him from 1568 to 1615. In 1611 his *Predictions* were printed alongside those of Nostradamus by Pierre Chevillot.

However, he came to a suitably dramatic end at the siege of Poussin, 1574. The grandmother of Louis XIV's wife, Mme. de Maintenon, describes it in her *Histoire Universelle* (1616–1620). "The abandoned town was exposed to pillage and even to fire by a very novel method. They had in the army a young Nostradamus, who claimed to be the son of Michel. Saint-Luc asked him what would happen to Poussin, and the young predictor, having thought for a long while, answered that it would perish by fire. During the pillage of the town this man was discovered, lighting fires everywhere." A soldier drove a lance through his stomach, and that was the end of his prophetic career. It is reminiscent of a man in fourth-century Greece who set fire to a monument so that his name might be remembered forever. The event was recorded, the name of the man forgotten.

In 1649, a false edition of the *Prophecies* was printed—dated 1568—with two additional quatrains added as a direct political attempt to lessen the power of Cardinal Mazarin in the French Court. They were cleverly inserted into the incomplete Century VII as quatrains 42 and 43 and then the real 42 as 44, etc. They run as follows:

1. *Quant Innocent tiendra le lieu de Pierre,*
   Le Nizaram cicilien (se verra
   En grands honneurs) mais après il cherra
   Dans le bourbier d'une civile guerre.

which translates—allowing for the very obvious pun in line 2, as follows:

When Innocent shall hold the place of Peter
The Sicilian Mazarin [Nizaram] will hold
Great honors, but after he will fall
In the mess of a civil war.

2.   *Latin in Mars, Sénateurs en Crédit,*
     Par une nuict Gaulle sera troublée.
     Du grand Croesus l'Horoscope prédit,
     Par Saturnus, sa puissance exilé.

     Latin in Mars, Senators in credit
     For one night Gaulle [France] will be troubled
     The horoscope of the great Croesus predicts
     His power in exile, through Saturn.

How effective these were as propaganda at the time is hard to tell. But the style, particularly of the first, is not that of Nostradamus. He never used brackets and the vocabulary and rhyming don't ring true, although the second verse is better than the first. Words such as Croesus and horoscope don't appear elsewhere in the *Prophecies*.

Another series of forgeries were the Prognostications, which first came to light in 1605. These were attributed to the would-be prophet, Michel le jeune. They were allegedly presented to Henri IV in that year by M. Sève, who was a grandson of Nostradamus. The dedication of the book is worthy of interest. He states that some years earlier he received certain Prognostications from an Henri Nostradamus, a nephew of the Prophet, written by Michel le jeune. He continues, "Since they concern the affairs of your state, particularly of your person and your successors, and since the truth of several of the sixains has already been borne out . . ."

One of the main circumstances which leads one to conclude that the Sixaines are a forgery is Sixaine 6.

> *Quand de Robin la traistreuse entreprise,*
> *Mettra Seigneurs en peine lui grand Prince,*
> *Sçeue par la Fin, chef on lui tranchera*
> *Le plume au vent, ayme dans Espagne*
> *Post attrapé estant dans la campagne,*
> *Et l'escrivain dans l'eauë se jettera.*

This translates as follows:

> *When the treacherous enterprises of Robin*
> *Will cause Lords and a Great Prince trouble,*
> *Known by Lafin, his head will be cut off.*
> *The feather in the wind, woman friend to Spain,*
> *The messenger trapped while in the country,*
> *And the writer will throw himself into the water.*

This refers only too clearly, with the minimum of punning on names, to the conspiracy of the Duc de Biron (Robin) against the king in 1602 and his resultant execution, the flight of his mistress and capture of documents sent to the Spanish king. It was obviously inserted early on in the Prognostications to give them authenticity. Although Sève states clearly that these apply only to the seventeenth century, many commentators have taken them up to the present day. I am however, in agreement with the major critics of Nostradamus' writings, such as Jaubert and Bareste, that they are forgeries, but who actually wrote them is unknown. It is interesting that they did not appear until approximately a year after the death of Chavigny, the only person who might have been able to disprove them.

During the unchronicled period of Nostradamus' wanderings after his first wife's death he is reputed to have stayed at the Cistercian Abbey at Orval in Belgian Luxembourg. Two poorly faked books of prophecies were allegedly discovered in the early nineteenth century, both in prose, not verse, predicting the coming of Napoleon. The first, *The Prophecy of Philip Olivarius 1542*, was probably, from analysis of the paper and printing processes, actually printed around 1800. The second, *The Prophecy of Orval 1544*, is probably a little later. Mlle. Le Normand, Napoleon's personal prophet, reports in her memoirs that Napoleon carried a copy of the first fake edition on his person wherever he went.

I have already discussed Hitler's imaginative use of Nostradamus' *Prophecies* after the suggestion was first made to him by Frau Dr. Goebbels.

However, by March 1940 it was apparent that all Dr. Goebbels wanted was propaganda material from stretched interpretations of Nostradamus— Krafft needed the money. There is an unverified assertion that by May he was involved in the preparation of leaflets dropped over France containing alleged prophecies by Nostradamus, designed to keep clear of refugees certain roads inside France

that the Germans wished to use. About the middle
of 1941 there was published in Belgium a book in
which Krafft discussed some forty quatrains in a
very pro-German manner. He and many other astrologers and similar characters were arrested by
the Gestapo in June 1941. Released for a time then
rearrested, Krafft died in January 1945, on the way
to a concentration camp.

Interestingly, distorted news of Krafft's activities
got through to England about March 1940, leading
to the appointment of an astrologer in England
who was supposed to work out the advice that
Hitler would have received. The British produced
some fake Nostradamus pamphlets, which were
smuggled into Germany, as were some impressively
printed booklets. "Nostradamus predicts the course
of the War," containing fifty bogus Nostradamus
quatrains and interpretations, mainly the work of
Sefton Delmar, who was almost certainly a complete charlatan.

Another rather less blameworthy example of
misuse was Steward Robb's *Nostradamus on
Napoleon, Hitler and the Present Crisis,* published in
1941, apparently based on a corrupt text. Two-
thirds of the book is about the quatrains relating to
Napoleon, on the whole reasonably interpreted. A
quarter of it is concerned with some twenty
quatrains believed to relate to the Second World
War; in my opinion some of the interpretations are
rather forced. It concludes with a very cursory examination of a further twenty quatrains relating to

the future, with little interpretation. They were not relevant to winning the war.

The defeat and destruction of a tyrant such as Hitler was without doubt a good political end, though I maintain that there was misuse of prophecy by both sides in the Second World War. It was a revelation to someone of my generation that this simplistic form of "black" warfare was still used.

Many prophets feel that to use their powers to bring about material gains for themselves or for others is a misuse, at best making them feel ill, at worst running the risk of losing their powers. Not all prophets believe that. Nostradamus died a wealthy man with his powers intact, but so far as can be discovered his wealth came from normal applications of intelligence as well as from the use of his predictive abilities.

Edgar Cayce was at times a victim of misuse. Once a New Yorker who had come to consult him left before Cayce came out of the trance in which he had been responding to questions. It turned out later that the New Yorker had got from him certain stock market predictions that turned out favorably which made Cayce believe, because he had felt so ill after the consultation, that to use his gifts for material gain was sinful. Thereafter he gave no further consultations except in the presence of his wife.

Some years later, he made many successful stock market forecasts for a New York financier, who used part of the proceeds to open a hospital for the treatment of patients whose illness Cayce had diagnosed in trance. He had signaled the collapse of the stock market in 1929, but his backer had not followed his advice, so the hospital failed financially. In 1931 he was arrested for fortune-telling. The charge was dismissed. Cayce felt discouraged, thinking that he had been punished for using his gift to obtain material gain, however purely motivated. He died in 1945, in comparative penury.

Summing up, exploitation of one's prophetic gifts for material gain does seem to be a misuse, either by diverting the energy that should have gone into more legitimate uses of those strange talents, or by losing the gift of prophecy all together. None of this means that a prophet has to remain poor, though there are perhaps more hazards for the "inspired" than for the "rational" prophet, for Edgar Cayce than for H. G. Wells, for instance.

Falsification of prophecies for good or bad ends is misuse, plain and simple. If a prophecy is favorable, to force it is to misuse it, and if it is unfavorable, then beware of letting it rule your conduct to the exclusion of all else.

12 IS PROPHECY DESIRABLE?

In one of the major points at the end of *Justine*, the first novel of *The Alexandria Quartet*, Lawrence Durrell writes of "a marriage of past and present with the flying multiplicity of the future racing towards one." I find two interesting things in that. This concept of the multiplicity of the future helps point to the value of prophecy, both inspired and rational, in helping us to see the possibilities more clearly and in choosing between them. A society where everything is predetermined by the laws of historical necessity or by the will of God or by the will of some dictator or by something else excludes prophecy. The early Christian church decreed that there should be no more prophets, though all the major denominations take a more relaxed attitude in these days. Under the Nazi régime astrological speculation about the life and well-being of Hitler was a serious crime. There is no place for prophecy in that bleak vision of the future of which *Brave New World* and *The Shape of Things to Come* show us different aspects. There is no place for it in the Soviet Union. It is probably no accident that the two most eminent inspired prophets of the past fifty years are American—Edgar Cayce and Jeane Dixon. I conclude that valid genuine prophecy is desirable in Western societies, though it is worth exploring a little the possibility that there are limits beyond which it can be undesirable, if not dangerous.

Perhaps we need to envisage a framework in which prophecy can operate more effectively. We could start by adapting something that Edmund Burke said about tolerance, and suggest that prophecy should not go so far as to endanger prophecy. We could look at some prophecies in the past which have had undesirable effects, at least from some points of view, and at other occasions where ignoring or misinterpretation of prophecies has led to difficulties.

Julius Caesar did not act upon the prediction by a soothsayer to beware the Ides of March, the day of his assassination. More direct warnings also came to Caesar but he set those aside too. Did he in some sense choose to die, or was his sense of personal security so strong that he felt able to ignore the prophecy and the other warnings? That assassination of a dictator who probably desired to be king was followed by many years of civil war. On balance, in my opinion, Rome lost by Caesar's assassination, so that the warning prophecy was desirable as well as correct.

In the Greek and Roman worlds prophecy was necessary rather than desirable. No decision on great affairs of state was made without attempting to get some kind of prediction of the effects of a particular line of action, for which the Greeks and for a time the Romans relied on oracles. It would be fair to describe the prophecies that came from those oracles as a varying mixture of inspiration and calculation. They were forbidden after the Roman Empire became Christian, but knowledge of the methods of divination survived in a few books that were rediscovered in the Renaissance, and came to the attention of Nostradamus in the sixteenth century.

When in 1518 the Spaniards first came into contact with the Aztec Empire in Mexico, the ruler Montezuma had already received warnings and prophecies of disaster to come. There was an old prophecy that their god Quetzalcoatl would return from the East. Many Mexican lords identified Cortez with their god. Such an identification facilitated the course of the Spanish conquest. Whether the effects of that particular prophecy were desirable or not is very much a matter of opinion and point of view—an empire destroyed versus more souls for Christ, more deaths from disease versus better living for the survivors. It seems clear that the existence of that particular prophecy tragically served to unnerve the Aztecs.

Reliable prophecies of natural and man-made disasters would certainly be desirable. The emphasis is on the word "reliable" and in this context premonitions, widely interpreted to take in dreams, visions, revelations and so on, is a more appropriate word than prophecies. In some cases predictions can be checked by scientific and technical studies. Natural disasters include such things as earthquakes, floods, forest fires, landslips, while man-made disasters include bombs, attacks by armies, train crashes; some occurrences such as shipwrecks belong in both groups.

A Central Premonitions Registry was founded in New York in 1968, and before that a Premonitions Registry was set up in London. Apart from registering predictions and using them in continuing investigation of the nature and accuracy of precognitions, such centers could develop into advance warning systems, especially for natural disasters. They need to base themselves initially on the predictions of a relatively large number of people who have established and verified records of success. There are difficulties. Very many predictions cannot be linked to specific disasters, for example, to a certain voyage of a particular ship, or to a specific flight number on a named date. The vast majority of disaster warnings will turn out to be false alarms. In principle this use of prediction must remain a desirable one, though whether it could ever be translated into practice is far from certain.

Inspired prophets such as Nostradamus have made many prophecies concerning earthquakes, about which there is also a considerable body of scientific knowledge, some of it modern and some of it dating back two thousand years and more in China. So much predictive work on earthquakes is going on by a mixture of precognitive and scientific methods, particularly in Japan and California, that it has almost become an industry in its own right. The aim is certainly desirable but the effectiveness is far from proven.

Accurate prophecies of dangers to eminent men and women are desirable provided appropriate warnings get through to the people concerned and provided that they or others take appropriate precautions. Julius Caesar ignored the prophecy. According to Jeane Dixon, who prophesied the assassination of President Kennedy, it was the will of God and could not have been avoided. How are police and security organizations to distinguish between reliable prophecies, threats, publicity seekers, mischief-makers and sincere but incompetent prophets? In genuine cases of real precognitive danger, how are the potential victims to be persuaded to protect themselves? The death of Mrs. Indira Gandhi is an extreme example of this. She refused to remove her Sikh bodyguards after repeated warnings and death threats.

I hope to provide some sort of preliminary outline of an answer, at least to the first question. The authorities should seek out, possibly through the Premonitions Registries described earlier in this chapter, a small number of people who do have reliable precognitive faculties for public persons. These people may rely for their knowledge on experiences in trance, as did Edgar Cayce, or on revelations, visions, vibrations from people and telepathy, as Jeane Dixon. There are not many such people. I do not think that I am one of them, for on the few occasions when I have felt imminent or future danger to someone with whom I was in contact, I have not been sufficiently sure of my despondent or gloomy feelings to translate them into warnings.

There is one kind of prophecy about whose desirability I must admit to having slight reservations, namely anything that has a kind of total finality about it. By this I mean such things as total destruction as the year 2000 approaches, Armageddon and universal war, the coming of the antichrist. I find these unacceptable, perhaps because they implicitly contain the kind of inevitability that believers in a free society should reject. I do not for one moment question the sincerity and honesty of those who make such predictions—among them Nostradamus and Jeane Dixon, as I have discussed in earlier chapters—but I have too much confidence in human beings' capacity for adaptation and survival. Yet a good case can be made for the desirability of such prophecies if they serve as terrible warnings of what *could* go wrong unless something changes or some desirable actions are taken. I have cited George Orwell's *1984* as a calculated rational prophecy that acts in this way, whether or not it is meant to do so, and I am sure that there are some inspired prophecies that are conditional in this way rather than absolute.

There are certain grounds on which almost any prophecy may be regarded as undesirable. It may paralyze action or distort judgment leading to wrong or foolish conduct, as happened to Macbeth. A prophecy may constrain a principal actor or participant to follow out his role exactly. The consequences of that are not always desirable. Prophecies can be seen as threats, sometimes rightly, to benevolent and useful organizations as well as to destructive and dictatorial bodies, secular or religious.

At their best prophecies provide an inspired guide to rational calculation, but they should always be interpreted cautiously. The philosopher George Santayana expressed the belief that those who would not learn from history were condemned to repeat it. Can I suggest that those who will not heed prophecy may be condemned to suffer from it?

One last but serious objection to the acceptance of prophecy. Is it compatible with a belief in free will? Personally I am sure that the two are compatible. The undoubted fact that those who are the most deterministic, the most convinced of the inevitability of certain religious or secular "laws" are the strongest opponents of prophecy is, I suggest, a strong argument in favor of the compatibility of free will and prophecy, provided one is not too absolute about either.

Start with a cyclical theory of time, allow loops in it, accept the "flying multiplicity of the future." Even if the absolute determinist position of Sir Thomas Browne is right, no one will ever know. Free will within wide limits is valid for human beings in free societies, whether or not it is an illusion or a glimpse of reality. But it is not *total* free will, or valid prophecy and prediction would be impossible. One knows that the future has not yet happened, and realists would say that there is no way in which one can see it all in a detailed perspective. The public predictions that form the major subject of this book are almost all about other people. Those who have proved their abilities to make valid predictions or prophecies, whether by inspiration or by rational calculation, such as John Dee, Nostradamus, J. W. Dunne, Jeane Dixon, Edgar Cayce, and H. G. Wells have not acted as though they believe in total predestination. My own personal experience does not lead me to reject a large measure of free choice and free will. Chaucer's "all that's preordained needs must be" is too extreme. I prefer Hamlet's "There are more things in heaven and earth, Horatio, Than are dreamt of in your philosophy."

What, if anything, can be done to create a framework in which prophecy and prediction can operate more effectively? Not much, I think, need be done to encourage the authors of rational calculated books on such subjects, except perhaps the institution of one or more annual prizes for such books. The Registries of Premonitions that I have referred to earlier in this chapter are doing a large amount of useful work in these fields, but mostly in what one might call the private rather than the public domain. Perhaps more could be done in the latter area of human experience and expectation. What, for instance?

Dare I go so far as to suggest the foundation of a Chair of Prophecy and Prediction at Oxford or Cambridge? In 1913 Oxford had Professors of Zen Philology, Pastoral Theology, Interpretation of Holy Scripture, Exegesis, Astronomy, Moral Philosophy (two), Divinity (two), Experimental Philosophy, among others. At the same time Cambridge had Professors of Mental Philosophy and Logic, Astrophysics, Astronomy (two) Divinity (no fewer than five), Moral Philosophy, Natural Philosophy, among others. Compared with these Chairs that existed a mere seventy years ago, a hardly perceptible length of time in the lives of the Universities of Oxford and Cambridge, my suggestion does not seem at all fanciful. A Chair of Prophecy and Prediction will occupy an independent area having frontiers with Literature, Astronomy, Natural Science, Philosophy, Psychology and Religion. Perhaps I shall see one in my lifetime.

What would be the subjects of study in a Department or School of Prophecy and Prediction? The main purpose would be the practical one of making prediction and prophecy more useful, accurate and reliable, especially the inspirational rather than the calculated aspects. It could provide a theoretical and intellectual framework within which to evaluate and improve the work of the Registries of Premonitions, and of such archives as those left by Edgar Cayce. It should find methods of locating those with prophetic gifts and of developing these gifts, as well as developing methods of evaluation. It could evolve theories of time to explain the possibility of valid prophecy, in part by studying it in action in other cultures and religions. That will do for a start.

What more need one say? There is a demand for knowledge in this field. I feel that opening up the field of prophecy is desirable, that prediction is possible, now, in the past and in the future, and we would be the better off for it.

After I had written this particular part of the book Arthur Koestler's will was published, leaving all his estate to any University which would establish a Chair for the study of the Paranormal. Cambridge refused immediately. Oxford at present vacillates. Three red-brick universities are said to be "seriously considering his offer." We shall see.

Erika Cheetham
September 1984
Paris

Index